Artist Profiles

Columbus, OH

The McGraw-Hill Companies

Photo Credits

SRAonline.com

SRA

Copyright © 2005 by SRA/McGraw-Hill.

Send all inquiries to:
SRA/McGraw-Hill
8787 Orion Place
Columbus, OH 43240-4027

Printed in the United States of America.

ISBN 0-07-601837-7

1 2 3 4 5 6 7 8 9 DBH 08 07 06 05 04

Table of Contents

Benny Andrews
b. 1930

Benny Andrews (ben´ ē an´ drūz) was born in rural Georgia during the Great Depression. His parents were farmers. They raised ten children. Andrews grew up watching his father George paint pictures on every available surface. Benny himself scratched pictures in the dirt with sticks. After high school, he served in the United States Air Force. At the time, Georgia did not permit African American students to attend its art schools. A federal law forced the state to pay part of Andrews's tuition to an out-of-state school. Andrews was able to earn a degree at the Art Institute of Chicago. But even there, the work of African American students was not included in student shows. After a long struggle, Andrews finally achieved recognition. His art now hangs in museums around the world, and he has taught and lectured at colleges across the nation.

About Art History

During the 1960s, Andrews led protests to have the art of African Americans exhibited. In 1982, he went to work for the National Endowment for the Arts, where he set up programs to help minority artists. He made sure they had many opportunities to show their work.

About the Artwork

Andrews's art, such as his *Southland Series,* focuses on people and places that were part of his southern upbringing. *Daydreams of a Young Boy* was inspired by his childhood desire to become a cowboy.

About the Media

Andrews is most recognized for his pen and ink drawings. In one of his early paintings, *Janitors at Rest,* he added paper towels and bathroom tissue. Since then he has often combined oils and collage.

About the Technique

Andrews often uses a neutral background to focus attention on his subject. He also uses actual articles in his paintings, such as a real blacksmith's apron in *The Blacksmith.*

Milton Avery
1893–1964

Milton Avery (mil´ tən ā´ və rē) was born in New York but grew up in Connecticut. He loved to paint and travel, and he also loved nature, landscapes, and color. Around 1905, Avery attended both the Connecticut League of Art Students in Hartford, Connecticut, and later the School of the Art Society in Hartford. Often he would paint all day long in his New York studio, sometimes creating five or six paintings or studies in a day. He established himself as a dedicated color field painter. He spent 50 years of his life painting, and created thousands of works of art.

About Art History

In 1925, after encountering the work of Matisse and Picasso, Avery began to simplify and abstract his own painting, although he never lost focus of representational subject matter. By the 1940s, he had eliminated almost all painted detail and was utilizing patterns of flattened shapes and arbitrary colors like Matisse. Avery's emphasis on color strongly influenced the work of younger artists, such as Rothko, Frankenthaler, Gottleib, and Newman, who were called color field painters. Avery was also a good friend of another American modernist, Hartley.

About the Artwork

Avery's paintings were said to combine modernism with folk art, a unique style for his time. By painting abstractly, Avery's use of color played an even larger role in his work, for it was expressive and suggested a subject. His use of color fields determined his portrayal of space and form, as in the painting *Mountain and Meadow*, where the spaces between simple mountains are created by a change in color.

About the Media

Most of Avery's numerous paintings were completed using oil on canvas. Because he generated so many paintings so swiftly, his sketches were usually outlined directly onto his canvases, although he did study figure drawing for a long time in art school.

About the Technique

Color field painters filled vast sections of their canvases with fields of color, sometimes using only a few hues to designate space or form. Avery applied his paint in large sections, simplifying the form of his subjects and using wide brushes to fill the canvas. For many of his paintings, he applied paint rapidly, which allowed him to experiment and create numerous paintings at one time.

Vladimir Baranoff-Rossine
1888–1944

Vladimir Baranoff-Rossine (vlə dē´ mir bə rä´ nəf rōs ēn´) was born in 1888 in Ukraine. He began his studies at Odessa and then attended the imperial Academie des Beaux Arts of St. Petersburg, Russia. When he was 22, Baranoff-Rossine relocated to Paris, France, where he began to exhibit his works professionally. During his time in Paris, his work evolved and became more geometric, a reflection of the creative impact of his friendship with other French cubist artists. After returning to St. Petersburg in 1917, he spent several years teaching art to pupils in his studio, married, and started a family. After returning to France with his wife and son in 1925, Baranoff-Rossine began to exhibit his work regularly at the Salon des Independants.

About Art History

Baranoff-Rossine was part of the Russian avant-garde art movement of the early twentieth century, which broke from traditional academic art and explored new experimental techniques. His work combined elements of the neoprimitive, cubist, and futurist movements of the time. One of his more famous contemporaries was the cubist painter Pablo Picasso. Art historians sometimes describe Baranoff-Rossine's style as *cubo-futurist* because his work displays the geometric, fragmented forms of cubism in brilliant harmony with the energy and motion of futurism.

About the Artwork

Baranoff-Rossine was passionate about combining color and sound in his art. This inspired him to create color music using a constructed optophonic piano, an instrument whose keys produced not only sound, but also color, which was instantly reflected on a screen. He made the optophone in 1914 and patented it in France. In addition to his paintings and color music Baranoff-Rossine created sculptures that expressed his avant-garde style. In *Symphony Number 1* he used slender, curving lines and geometric, abstract forms to depict a human figure.

About the Media

The paintings of Baranoff-Rossine were typically created with pencil and oil paints on canvas. He used polychrome in some of his sculptures, including *Symphony Number 1.*

About the Technique

Sometimes Baranoff-Rossine created preliminary studies and sketches of his paintings, and other times he intuitively applied paint or pencil to canvas without a clear composition in mind.

Romare Bearden
1911–1988

Romare Bearden (rō mar´ bēr dən) was born in North Carolina. His family moved to Harlem in New York City when he was three years old. His family's home became a meeting place for artists, writers, and musicians during the Harlem Renaissance. Bearden studied math, not the arts, in college, but he worked as a cartoonist and illustrator to pay for it. When he was 21, he decided to become a professional artist. Over the years, Bearden studied art in New York City and Paris, France. He also worked as a social worker, served in the army, and wrote several songs and books. Bearden was known as a warmhearted, friendly man.

About Art History

Bearden experimented with abstract expressionism. He later developed his own style and created collages combining painting and photographs. He often showed his subjects at odd angles in a style similar to cubism.

About the Artwork

Bearden focused much of his work on African American life. His subjects were inspired by the legends of Homer, jazz and other music, and religion. Bearden's later paintings show scenes and colors from the West Indies. His wife's family lived there, and the Beardens visited often.

About the Media

Bearden was a painter and printmaker. He began by painting with tempera on brown paper, the kind of paper used for grocery bags. Later Bearden used watercolors, oils, and acrylics. He incorporated photographic images in his paintings.

About the Technique

Some of Bearden's paintings include magazine photographs pieced together like a quilt. Other times, he painted on several layers of rice paper. Then he tore away some sections and added others. He continued to tear and paint until he had created the picture he wanted.

John Biggers
1924–2000

John Biggers (jon big´ ərs) was born in South Carolina. He was the youngest of seven children. Biggers greatly admired his father, who had lost a leg as a child while working at a plantation sawmill. As an adult, his father became the principal of a three-room school. To pay his own tuition at a private school, Biggers got up every morning at 4 A.M. to start the school's furnaces. After graduating, he began to paint. In 1943, Biggers was drafted into World War II. He soon discovered that African American soldiers were shown less respect than German prisoners of war. He became so depressed that he was hospitalized. In time Biggers went back to school and earned his degree at Pennsylvania State University. Later he taught art and set up art departments at several colleges. In 1957, he traveled to Africa to study art.

About Art History

Biggers was strongly influenced by the internationally famous art educator Viktor Lowenfeld, who had escaped from the Nazis during World War II. Lowenfeld encouraged his students to use art to express the disappointment and joy in their lives. After a trip to Africa, Biggers focused on African traditions and symbols. He was one of the first African American artists to become well known. His murals grace buildings across the United States.

About the Artwork

Biggers's work focuses on human themes. At first he painted memories from his childhood and scenes of urban poverty, such as *Victim of the City Streets.* Later he recorded many aspects of African life. He wrote and illustrated a book about his African journey, *"Ananse: The Web of Life."*

About the Media

Biggers worked in pencils, oils, and tempera. He also sculpted.

About the Technique

Before beginning a mural Biggers sketched his subjects. He did careful research so he could make his images exact. While working, he listened to inspiring African spirituals and African American speeches.

Teodora Blanco
1928–1980

Teodora Blanco (tā´ ō dôr ä blän´ kō) was born in a poor village in Mexico where little girls were required to learn to make pots. Their plain but useful pots were sold to help support the family. Unlike many of her playmates, Blanco loved to work with clay. When she went to the market to sell her pots, she also stopped at the museum to study the artwork there. In time, she began to decorate her pots with figures. Blanco's unique pots sold well, so she was encouraged to experiment with her figures.

As she became a recognized artist, Blanco took an active role in her community, helping families in need as well as encouraging young potters. Now three of her five children carry on the family pottery tradition. As they fill orders sent in from around the world, they work in the style their mother developed. Nelson Rockefeller was one of Blanco's admirers and bought her work for museum collections.

About Art History

As a self-taught artist Blanco began sculpting with clay in a simple folk art style. One early example is *Market Woman,* which shows a native woman carrying pots she hopes to sell. Gradually Blanco shifted to an elaborate rococo style, such as *Kangaroo Rat,* which shows a sculpture of a figure covered with floral designs.

About the Artwork

Blanco expressed the myths and beliefs of her heritage in clay. She created human and animal figures as spirits to protect people. She often combined human and animal characteristics in one figure, which might be as tall as 30 inches. Blanco covered many of her figures with flowers as symbols of fertility, which was so important to families that depend on farming. She also created scenes of animals playing musical instruments, reminiscent of musicians in her village.

About the Media

Blanco worked entirely with clay.

About the Technique

Blanco, like her children today, created her pots and figures on a covered porch behind her simple home. She fired them in a homemade kiln and stored them in huts with thatched roofs.

Pieter Bruegel the Elder

1525–1569

Pieter Bruegel (pē´ ter broi gǝl) the Elder was born in Holland. He studied art in Antwerp, Belgium, and later married his teacher's daughter. They had two sons, who also became painters. Pieter the Younger was a portrait painter. The other son, Jan, painted flowers. Bruegel the Elder was educated and wealthy. However, he often dressed like a poor farmer so that he could closely observe the lives of peasants. He made them the subjects of many of his paintings. Bruegel even attended weddings of strangers. He brought gifts so that he would be welcome. Bruegel died at age 44.

About Art History

Bruegel began his painting career during the Renaissance. Many Renaissance artists created portraits that showed their subjects as heroes. Bruegel chose to paint ordinary people engaged in everyday activities.

About the Artwork

Bruegel was interested in the changing seasons and often focused on them in his landscapes. One example is *Hunters in the Snow.* Some people think it is the greatest landscape painting ever made. Bruegel also loved to paint peasants enjoying games and celebrations. One book of his paintings, *Children's Games,* shows at least eighty games of the time. Some of Bruegel's paintings served as warnings. *The Parable of the Blind* warns viewers against following others blindly.

About the Media

Bruegel worked in oils and pen and ink. Some of his works were made into engravings. Engravings are pictures transferred to paper from metal plates.

About the Technique

Bruegel drew pictures of his subjects. Then he combined bits and pieces from his drawings to create a painting. Bruegel most often focused on the subjects' actions.

Emily Carr
1871-1945

Emily Carr (em´ ə lē kär) was born in British Columbia, Canada. She liked to paint and draw as a child, but her family did not encourage her. Her parents died when she was a teenager. Struggling to establish herself as an artist, she taught art, grew fruit, raised animals, and made pottery and rugs.

Carr visited many Native American reservations. She admired the people and their art and used them as subjects in her paintings. The head of an art museum in Ottawa recognized her skills. Carr later met the Group of Seven—young Canadian artists who were experimenting with painting. At last she belonged to a community and began to paint full time. Carr was in her late 60s before she made a living from her art. When heart attacks slowed her down, she turned to writing. Her books, including her autobiography *Growing Pains*, became even more popular than her paintings.

About Art History

Carr developed a unique painting style. She was influenced by the two years between 1910 and 1912 she spent in France. After that trip, she began to paint in an impressionistic style. She used forceful brushstrokes and strong colors, and her art showed energy.

About the Artwork

Carr focused mostly on two subjects—indigenous people of the Canadian west coast and the rain forests of British Columbia. Her paintings document a way of life that has since disappeared.

About the Media

Carr worked in watercolors and oils.

About the Technique

To save money Carr sometimes used cheap paper and white house paint thinned with gasoline. She loved to paint outdoors where the view was "fresh." Carr often painted the same scene in the morning, after lunch, and in the early evening to work with different angles of light. Some critics consider these quick paintings her best work.

Marc Chagall
1887–1985

Marc Chagall (mark sha gäl´) was born in a small town in Russia, Vitebsk, which is now part of Belarus. He studied art in Saint Petersburg and then in Paris, France. After the Russian revolution he served as the director of the art academy in his hometown. From 1919 to 1922, Chagall was the art director of the Moscow Jewish State Theater. He painted murals in the theater lobby and created sets for the shows. In 1923, he moved to France. He spent most of the rest of his life there, except for a brief period of residence in the United States from 1941 to 1948.

About Art History

Chagall was one of the first people to paint pictures that looked like dreams. For example, he created many paintings of animals and people flying through the air, sometimes upside down. Chagall is sometimes referred to as an early surrealist because of his dreamlike style and the element of fantasy in his work.

About the Artwork

Born into a very religious Jewish family, Chagall's work shows the strong influence of his home and his heritage. He included childhood memories and religious images in his work. His work combines memories with folklore and fantasy. Chagall created 12 stained-glass windows for the Hadassah Hospital in Jerusalem, Israel, illustrating the Old Testament. He created canvas murals for the ceiling of the Opera in Paris, in addition to two large canvas murals for the lobby of the Metropolitan Opera House in New York City.

About the Media

Chagall usually worked in oils on canvas. He also created stained-glass windows, and designed costumes for ballet dancers.

About the Technique

Chagall often remembered things from his childhood and drew them on canvas. He covered whole canvases with many pictures of different sizes. He sometimes drew people with just one big eye or animals that looked like monsters. He painted them in bright colors, such as red, blue, and yellow.

Chief Black Hawk
c. 1830–1890

Plains Indian artist Chief Black Hawk (blak hôk) was a member of the Lakota tribe of the Sans Arc band who lived on the Cheyenne River Sioux Reservation. He was a medicine man who acted as a mediary between his Lakota people and the non-Lakota domain, and he used his artwork to express the strength and heritage of his culture. While the Plains Indians were fighting for their land and independence Black Hawk created commissioned drawings of his people, which served to explain their world to outside forces. His numerous sketches addressed the ceremonial, spiritual, and physical aspects of the Lakota, and provided a means for their world to be remembered in history.

▲ **Chief Black Hawk.** (American).
Crow Men in Ceremonial Dress. c. 1880–1881.

Ink and pencil on paper. $10\frac{1}{2} \times 16\frac{1}{4}$ inches (26 × 41.9 cm.). Fenimore Art Museum, Cooperstown, New York.

About Art History

William Edward Caton, a Cheyenne Agency trader in 1880, commissioned Black Hawk's sketches of the Lakota people. He supplied the artist with pencils and paper and paid him 50 cents for each sheet of drawing, which was a considerable sum of money at the time. There is little known about the drawings' whereabouts in the later twentieth century, but Black Hawk's sketchbook was discovered in a file cabinet and eventually brought to auction in the 1990s. The drawings were later donated to the Fenimore Art Museum in Cooperstown, New York, where they remain today.

About the Artwork

Other native artists like Black Hawk concentrated on depicting the forts, armies, and interaction between expansionists and Native Americans, but Black Hawk chose instead to ignore the approaching outside world. In his sketches, he maintained the independence of his culture by representing its tradition alone. One of his drawings, *Crow Men in Ceremonial Dress,* expresses this tradition and gives the viewer an intimate and honest look at the ceremonial practices of Black Hawk's heritage. Like other Lakota artwork during this period, Black Hawk's work does not incorporate background or ground line, but pays attention to small details made by delicate lines of pencil.

About the Media

Black Hawk used pencil and paper for his sketches, which were then bound in a book.

About the Technique

Black Hawk relied on personal observation and experience to create his drawings. He did not have any conventional or formal artistic training.

Chryssa
b. 1933

Born and educated in Greece, Chryssa (kris´ ə) first studied social work but redirected her career path, because she felt that many relief funds ignored people in need. She studied in Athens, Paris, and California, and began her artistic career as a sculptor in New York during the 1950s. Her exploration of neon light and commercial signs was a new combination of materials to the art scene and opened up many avenues for her public installations. Chryssa does her own metalwork and the physical labor required by her art. She is regarded as highly motivating by her coworkers.

About Art History

Chryssa's assemblage sculptures and concentration on form are a reaction against the widespread abstract expressionism of the 1950s. Instead of focusing purpose, she emphasizes the actual materials and signs of her artwork, drawing attention to their shapes and functions. In her earlier work she used pop images and letters of the alphabet, which set the stage for other pop artists, such as Jasper Johns and Andy Warhol.

About the Artwork

In her earlier work, Chryssa's sculptures featured commercial signs and lettering and were inspired by the teeming energy of New York's Times Square. Her first major work, *Times Square Sky*, was a turning point for her, as it was her first use of neon light. In many of her pieces, Chryssa relies on the reflective surfaces of metal to reverberate the glowing neon light as shown in her piece *Americanoom*.

About the Media

Stainless steel, welded steel, aluminum, neon, Plexiglas, signs, and flashing lights all come into play in Chryssa's artwork. Sometimes the lettering and lights are interwoven to create a bombarding force of visual stimuli that can be both overpowering and intriguing at the same time. This barrage of information is intended to evoke a wide range of emotion from her viewers—from fear to joy—just as one might feel if suddenly surrounded by an overflow of noise and bright lights.

About the Technique

Much of Chryssa's work incorporates welded steel and aluminum, which she manipulates and finishes herself, although some of her pieces use glass obtained from glassblowers or foundries. One of her major creations uses a timer that turns the neon lights on and off, and all of her sculptures require precise measurements and an understanding of electrical connections to be successful.

John Singleton Copley

1738–1815

John Singleton Copley (jän sing´ gəl tən kä´ plē) was born in Boston one year after his parents arrived from Ireland. His father died, and his mother supported the family by running a tobacco shop. When Copley was 11, his mother married Peter Pelham, who was a printmaker, a painter, and a teacher. Pelham quickly saw young Copley's talent and gave him his first art lessons. Copley also learned from studying prints of paintings by Michelangelo, Raphael, and Rubens. In 1774, he was encouraged to go to Europe to study. He left his family in Boston and toured Europe. His father-in-law was one of the importers of the famous shipment of tea that was dumped in Boston Harbor. Because of that incident, his father-in-law left the Colonies in anger, taking Copley's wife and children with him to London. Copley also went to London, where he enjoyed brief success.

About Art History

Copley was one of the finest American artists of colonial times. In his early paintings, Copley wanted to show people as they were. His paintings were said to be "more real than real." After he moved to England, his work was influenced by British and other European painters. It lost some of its energy and realism.

About the Artwork

Among Copley's early portraits were those of such American patriots as Paul Revere and John Hancock. He also painted English patriots who opposed America's independence. After moving to England, Copley began painting dramatic historical events.

About the Media

Copley worked primarily in oils.

About the Technique

Copley brought life to his early paintings by including objects used by his subjects in their daily lives. He was especially skillful at depicting his subjects' eyes. Through their eyes, he tried to show their characters. At first his art was appreciated and earned high prices. But he was not used to painting a portrait in one five hour session, as was the custom in London, and he soon fell out of fashion. His life ended on a sad note; he was in debt and lonely for his life in America.

Salvador Dalí
1904–1989

Salvador Dalí (sal´ və dôr dä lē´) was born in Spain and grew up in a prosperous family. During his childhood he spent summers in a small coastal village in Spain, where his parents built his first studio, and many of his paintings portray his love of that area. Dalí earned fame and recognition early in his career with exhibitions in both Europe and the United States, and he continued to receive attention throughout his career, which spanned many styles and artistic experiments. Dalí was a surrealist, and he considered his paintings to be "dream photographs." He explored many different techniques and materials which influenced the surrealist movement everywhere. He moved to America and then Spain, where he opened the Teatro Museo.

About Art History

Surrealism was founded by the French writer André Breton, who was involved in the Paris Dada movement after World War I. He believed that art should free human behavior, so he published his *Manifesto of Surrealism* that expressed the necessity of humans to liberate their unconscious and communicate their personal desires. In 1928, Dalí joined this group of surrealists and took part in dream analysis, free association, automatic writing, word games, and hypnotic trances in order to discover the larger reality, or "surreality," beyond everyday ideas of rational logic. He swiftly became the leader of the surrealist movement, which included artists such as Joan Miró, André Masson, and Max Ernst.

About the Artwork

The Persistence of Memory is based on Dalí's childhood memory of a doctor asking to see his tongue. Melting watches drip over a tree limb and table, and a fleshy, alien creature draped at the painting's center is a grotesque image of Dalí's own profile with a limp tongue protruding from his nose. Ants, a representation of the passage of time, attack a pocket watch and symbolize decay in a dreamlike landscape. This painting is one of the most celebrated paintings of the twentieth century and combines reality and dreams, landscape and technology, and the symbolic and the irrational.

About the Media

Dalí worked in many media, including oil paints, watercolors, and pen and ink. He also created sculpture.

About the Technique

Sometimes Dalí relied on dreams to provide subject matter for his paintings, and he referenced the theories of Sigmund Freud in his painted explorations of personal fears and fantasies.

Stuart Davis
1894–1964

Stuart Davis (stū´ ərt dā´ vəs) was born in Philadelphia. He left high school when he was only 16 years old and went to New York City to study art. His long career began when he showed some paintings in the Armory Show in New York City in 1913. This large and important show introduced modern art to many Americans. Afterward Davis's career took off. By the 1920s, he was studying cubism. Through the 1940s, many of his paintings showed his love of jazz music. He even gave some of his paintings musical titles.

About Art History

Cubism is a style of art first developed by Pablo Picasso and Georges Braque in the early 1900s. The cubists simplified forms into basic geometric shapes. This style influenced Davis, and he, too, simplified objects into flat-looking, colored shapes.

About the Artwork

Davis was interested in city scenes with many people and factories. He painted pictures of streets in Manhattan and Paris using colorful, geometric shapes. He also painted dense canvases full of many abstract forms. Sometimes he reworked the same picture several times to explore different ways of arranging and coloring the shapes. Often his unusual signature is part of the composition.

About the Media

Davis generally worked in oils on canvas.

About the Technique

Davis began by making many drawings of what he was going to paint. Each time, he simplified the shape. After drawing the shapes on the canvas, he painted them in bright, solid colors.

Charles Edenshaw
1839-1924

Charles Edenshaw (chärlz ē′ dən shô) was born on Prince of Wales Island, British Columbia. For more than 200 years Haida artists such as Edenshaw have been carving argillite sculptures. Edenshaw married Isabella K'woiyang, and they had seven children. When his two young sons died, Edenshaw sought comfort by teaching young carvers. Some of these young students went on to become noted Haida carvers. Edenshaw earned a reputation as an artist and was noticed by anthropologists and museum collectors who were determined to record and collect Haida art. In the 1890s, their interest offered Edenshaw a great opportunity to produce even more of his traditional carvings and to establish a name for himself outside of Canada.

About Art History

Edenshaw began carving at the age of 14 when he became bedridden due to an illness. He went on to apprentice with his uncle, Albert Edward Edenshaw, a successful Haida artist. Learning from a family member was customary in Haida culture, and Edenshaw's uncle taught him how to perfect his carving technique and skills. By the 1880s, Edenshaw was supporting his family completely through his art. Most artists during his time needed to supplement their careers with hunting or fishing.

About the Artwork

The argillite sculptures of today represent the ancient traditions and myths of Haida culture. Edenshaw's *Model Totem Pole* incorporates Haida myths with its inclusion of animal storytelling figures. Edenshaw's work is characterized by bold lines and forms, as seen in the stylized finish and clean, rounded form of his totem pole. The detail with which he carved the fish scales and bird feathers is indicative of his master craftsmanship,

especially given the relatively small height of the totem pole.

About the Media

Edenshaw worked in wood, argillite, and precious metals and became known for his jewelry, totem poles, and functional sculptures. Most of his creations were custom-crafted argillite carvings for tourists. *Argillite* is a slate rock found on Slatechuck Mountain on the Queen Charlotte Islands in British Columbia.

About the Technique

Each animal or figure in a totem pole plays a necessary part in its overall narrative. The placement and order of each figure is important. Edenshaw mapped out a plan before carving the final creation. Like many carvers and sculptors, he created a smaller, three-dimensional model before creating the larger work of art.

Eliot Elisofon
1911–1973

Born in New York, Eliot Elisofon led a richly multifaceted life, primarily as a photographer and photojournalist. He worked for *LIFE* and *National Geographic,* created television productions, and was a war photographer and correspondent. He traveled throughout six continents, completing assignments on architecture, celebrities, food, African life, and social subjects. In addition to photography he was a color consultant for films, a painter of watercolors, and a famous collector of primitive art. He shared his knowledge with others by lecturing at museums, colleges, and clubs around the country, and wrote many essays, articles, and books about his experiences.

About Art History

Once Elisofon decided to make photography his career he opened a commercial photo studio in 1935 with Marty Bauman and Al Weiner. From there he moved to fashion photography and later, documentary photography. Elisofon traveled during the end of World War II to document life on the warfront. For three decades after the war he was connected with dozens of projects around the world, as well as the film, movie, and television industries.

About the Artwork

Elisofon was interested in African culture and a wide body of his photographic work is from his travels there. He would often photograph people working at their daily jobs, documenting their lives through his camera. He also took part in a number of documentary filming expeditions that took him to places such as the South Pacific and New Guinea. His fashion photographs were of a different, intentionally posed nature, and were printed in *Mademoiselle, Vogue,* and *Glamour.*

About the Media

For his photographs Elisofon created silver gelatin prints and used a variety of cameras.

About the Technique

When Elisofon photographed portraits or works of art he spent a great deal of time setting up specific lightings and backgrounds, much like some painters make preliminary sketches. When he was on assignment, he had a split second to capture an image on film. These spontaneous moments made it important for Elisofon to always be aware of his environment and to always have his camera ready. He also needed to have an accurate understanding of light and color, because his work found him in many places where he relied solely on outdoor natural light.

Minnie Evans
1890–1987

Minnie Evans (min´ ē ev´ ənz) was born in North Carolina. She left the state only once in her life. She went to school through the sixth grade, and had no training in art. Yet she said, "Something told me to draw or die." She started drawing in 1925 and continued for the rest of her life. Evans first used crayons and later created collages. All of her work expressed her vision of the relationship between God, people, and nature. She worked as a maid and a gatekeeper at Airlie Gardens in Wilmington, North Carolina. Her art hangs in the permanent collections of museums as far away as Switzerland.

About Art History

Evans used the colors of Caribbean folk art and the complex designs seen in Byzantine mosaics. Her work might be considered surreal, as her drawings came from her visions, not from seeing other artwork or studying art styles.

About the Artwork

Evans often drew a human face in a garden paradise. She wanted to show that God is in nature through the blaze of colors. The time Evans spent at Airlie Gardens inspired her to paint the brilliant flowers and lush plants that fill her work. One of her best-known collages, *Design Made at Airlie Gardens,* overflows with faces and plants.

About the Media

Evans worked in oils, watercolors, pencil, pen and ink, crayon, and collage.

About the Technique

Evans said she never planned a drawing or painting; it just happened for her. She simply transferred the vision in her mind to paper. Sometimes she reused earlier drawings by pasting them onto cardboard or canvas and then combined them with new designs in oils and watercolors.

Audrey Flack
b. 1931

Audrey Flack (ô´ drē flak) grew up in New York City and lives there still. She earned a fine arts degree from Yale. She also studied anatomy, the structure of the human body. This helps her make her paintings more realistic. Flack is married to a musician. Early in her career she painted while raising two daughters. She has also taught at Pratt Institute and New York University.

▲ **Audrey Flack.** (American). *Self-Portrait (The Memory).* 1958.

Oil on canvas. 50 × 34 inches (127 × 86.36 cm.).
Art Museum Miami University, Oxford, Ohio.

About Art History

Flack was a leader of the photorealists in the 1970s. She was one of the first artists to base paintings on photographs. However, she has also created abstract art. In fact, she does not follow any one art style. Instead, she paints and sculpts from her heart. She likes to reinvent her subjects in new ways.

About the Artwork

Flack has painted large abstract images, smaller realistic still lifes, portraits, landscapes, and seascapes. She has also created photorealistic paintings based on news stories. An example is *Kennedy Motorcade,* which focuses on the day President Kennedy was killed. Flack sometimes includes images of herself in her art. For instance, she placed a photo of herself in a painting of Marilyn Monroe. Her work often focuses on issues that are important to her, such as the role of women in society. Since 1983, Flack has focused on her sculpting because she likes its solid feel. Many of her sculptures look like ancient Greek goddesses in modern settings.

About the Media

Flack works in oils, acrylics, watercolors, and bronze sculpture.

About the Technique

In her photorealistic work Flack painted from slides projected onto canvas. At one time she used commercial slides and postcards. Later she worked from color slides she took herself. She uses an airbrush to apply paint.

Viola Frey
b. 1933

Viola Frey (vī ō´ lə frī) was born in Lodi, California, on a farm and vineyard. She grew up with strong female role models and became a collector of found objects. She especially likes collecting little figurines from flea markets, and she inserts these objects into ceramic assemblage artwork. These sculptures represent the way the modern world has come to depend on material goods. Frey's large ceramic human figures also reference or critique the modern world and are often covered with symbols and textures that give them an appearance similar to assemblage.

About Art History

Frey studied painting with Richard Diebenkorn at the California College of Arts and Crafts, then focused on ceramics at Tulane University, where she studied with Katherine Choy. In 1958, she went with Choy to the New York Clay Art Center, where she pursued her studies in sculpture, but realized that the center for the ceramic movement was on the west coast. She moved back to California and became interested in the figurative movement practiced by artists such as Diebenkorn and Joan Brown. In the 1980s Frey began making her famous monumental human sculptures that now reside in public and private collections around the world.

About the Artwork

Frey is predominantly a sculptor and enjoys creating works that represent the human figure. Grandmothers, spirals, figurines, horses, businessmen, monsters, the mind, the world, age, beauty, and ugliness are just some of the subjects and themes of her work. She often sculpts monumental figures of women or men in business suits, creating them in such a large scale that they seem to tower over viewers like adults peering down at children. To Frey, her larger-than-life women represent the self-determination and authority of all women and serve as an avenue of social critique. The energetic brushwork and brightly colored symbols adorning her figurative sculptures further emphasize their strength, as seen in her ceramic piece *Family Portrait.*

About the Media

Both Frey's large and small sculptures are ceramic creations. Some are hand-built, and others are slip-cast. Frey also makes drawings, assemblages, and decorative, biographical ceramic plates.

About the Technique

It takes Frey about a year to complete a monumental figurative sculpture. She paints energetic symbols with energetic colors. For her assemblages, Frey accumulates lots of found objects over time and assembles them into a sculpture or work of art, relying on the combined meaning of all the objects to give the final piece its identity.

Paul Gauguin
1848–1903

As one of France's leading postimpressionist painters, the artistic career of Paul Gauguin (pôl gō gan´) did not begin until he was a 25-year-old stockbroker. He decided to become a painter when he saw the first impressionist exhibit in Paris, France, in 1874, and throughout the next 30 years he developed his own style independent from impressionism and full of influences and experiences from his life. He was not content or fulfilled in Europe, however, and in 1891 he left his family and job to move to Tahiti and various other destinations in the South Pacific. With the exception of a two-year absence, Gauguin remained in Tahiti for the rest of his life, painting until his death in 1903.

About Art History

Through his encounters and friendship with van Gogh, Pissarro, and Cézanne, Gauguin developed a passion for expression through color. In the 1880s, he painted in France and created landscapes similar to those of Pissarro.

About the Artwork

Gauguin's style is a conceptual method of representation. His subjects, mainly women, are painted in flat, bold colors emphasizing a wild, almost untamed environment. His exposure to primitive art in Tahiti can clearly be seen in the rich colors in pieces such as *Faaturuma*. A woman's surroundings are painted in bright, earthy tones and her dress is a warm rose color that brings her image even closer to the viewer. Gauguin's ties with impressionism were, at this point, behind him. He had finally found his own style in a new land.

About the Media

Gauguin's portraits were created in oils on canvas. When he painted in France, he also used pastels for some of his landscapes.

About the Technique

The colorful, flat appearance of Gauguin's paintings was achieved by using large brushes and brushstrokes. Many of his paintings were created by sketching and studying models, and the expressive nature of his surfaces reflects the influence of the primitive art of the South Pacific.

Natalya Sergeevna Goncharova
1881–1962

Natalya Goncharova (nä täl´ē ä gon´ chä rō vä) was a member of the second generation of Russian women to receive art education. She became a leader of this generation of artists, taking part in the social, political, and aesthetic upheavals of the early twentieth century. After studying history and science—as well as sculpture and painting in Moscow—Goncharova joined other avant-garde artists in developing new forms of Russian art. They used native Russian peasant art, religious icons, and traditional folk culture in their work. She exhibited her paintings until the end of her life.

▲ **Natalya Sergeevna Goncharova.** (Russian). *Self-Portrait with Yellow Lillies.* 1907.

Oil on canvas. Iretyakov Gallery, Moscow, Russia.

About Art History

Early in her career, Goncharova joined with modern Russian painters Mikhail Larionov and David Burliuk to create Russian neo-primitivism. Neo-primitivism was among the new art forms that took hold after 1910. The changes produced in painting and sculpture by Goncharova and her colleagues strongly influenced twentieth-century art.

About the Artwork

Goncharova always strived to show the viewer how she structured her images. She also worked on theater and ballet designs and left Russia to create décor and costumes for the Ballet Russes in Paris, France. In 1917, she settled permanently in Paris and continued to design for theater.

About the Media

Goncharova worked with gouache. *Gouache* is an opaque watercolor paint similar to the tempera paint used in schools. It covers the paper with a smooth, matte coat.

About the Technique

Goncharova used bright colors and intense contrasts inspired by Russian folk and religious art, indigenous fabric, and furniture designs.

Paul Goodnight

b. 1946

Paul Goodnight (paul gud´ nīt) was born in Chicago and raised by his grandparents in New London, Connecticut. As a child he was happy but often in trouble. After serving in the Vietnam War, Goodnight was so devastated he could no longer speak clearly. He turned to painting and drawing as a way to work through the horrors he experienced during the war. After earning a bachelor's degree from Massachusetts College of Art, Goodnight worked as a commercial artist, creating album covers and package designs. His art has become very popular and has been featured on movie and television sets, including *The Fresh Prince of Bel Air, Seinfeld,* and *ER.* One of Goodnight's images was chosen for an Olympics poster.

About Art History

Goodnight's work shows the influence of his travels to Haiti, Nicaragua, Brazil, Russia, Senegal, and other nations.

About the Artwork

Goodnight focuses on ethnic images that communicate his pride in his African heritage. These images have been printed in many forms, from refrigerator magnets to book illustrations. His portraits tend to be combinations of faces he has seen rather than of specific people. Many of Goodnight's figures seem to look directly at viewers.

About the Media

Skilled in a variety of media, Goodnight uses pencils, oils, pastels, acrylics, and stained glass.

About the Technique

Goodnight works by building layers on a canvas. He uses free-flowing movements and often includes hot colors, such as magenta and bright orange.

Duane Hanson
1925–1996

Duane Hanson (dwān han´ sən) carved little figures out of logs using kitchen knives as a boy in his native Minnesota. Later he attended art school and taught art in Atlanta, Georgia and Miami, Florida. The same art dealer who discovered Andy Warhol arranged for Hanson's first solo exhibition. His life-size sculptures of ordinary people were an immediate success with the public. People could identify with his work. Hanson married and had five children. He continued to plan and create sculpture until the end of his life.

About Art History

Hanson's super-realistic style is so successful that people try to start conversations with his sculptures. One time a museum visitor dialed 911 to get help for an "unconscious" Hanson sculpture.

About the Artwork

Hanson created more than 100 sculptures during his career. His subjects were real people, ranging from janitors to sunbathers to athletes. One example is *Tourists,* a life-size and lifelike man and woman dressed in clashing clothing. Hanson's aim was to make viewers more aware of themselves and others. In a lighthearted way he tried to warn viewers not to want so much that they can never be happy.

About the Media

Hanson used a combination of polyester resin and fiberglass to create his sculptures.

About the Technique

Hanson often took six weeks or more to construct a sculpture. He began by choosing a model, often one of his friends. He posed the person and covered the model's body with petroleum jelly to keep the mold from sticking to the skin. He formed the mold by applying plaster bandages to parts of the model until he had made a mold of the model's whole body. After each mold dried and hardened, he removed it. Then he filled the plaster mold with a flesh-colored mixture of polyester resin and fiberglass to form the sculpture. After reassembling the parts, he painted the figure. Finally he added glass eyes, clothing, a wig, and accessories.

Martin Johnson Heade
1819–1904

Martin Johnson Heade (mär´ tən jän´ sən hed) was born in rural Pennsylvania, and led a long and varied artistic career. His early career in portraits gave way to landscapes in the mid-nineteenth century and established him as a leading luminist painter. He was well-traveled, moving from city to city in search of subject matter. He finally found inspiration in the constantly changing forms of landscape painting.

▲ **Thomas Hicks.** (American). *Martin Johnson Heade.* 1841.

Oil on canvas. $35\frac{5}{8} \times 31\frac{11}{16}$ inches (89.53 × 79.43 cm.). Collection of the Mercer Museum of the Bucks County Historical Society, Doylestown, Pennsylvania.

About Art History

In the beginning of Heade's career he studied portrait painting with the Quaker painters Edward and Thomas Hicks. By the 1840s, he had established his standing as a skilled portraitist and began exhibiting on the east coast. In 1859, he moved to New York where he met his friend Frederick Edwin Church and turned from portraits to landscapes. Heade was associated primarily with luminism, and his fellow luminist painters included George Caleb Bingham and William Sydney Mount.

About the Artwork

Characteristics of luminism are simplified color, intensified light, and still silence. Although he was frequently allied with the Hudson River School styles, Heade did not completely employ their grandiose depiction or celebration of nature's imposing vastness. Instead he chose to paint quieter, deeper scenes and was well-known for his compositions of marshes and shores. The bays and salt marshes around Rhode Island were often inspiration for his paintings, and he painted a number of his works in series. In 1863, he made the first of three trips to South America, where he became fascinated with hummingbirds and small tropical scenes. He maintained this interest throughout the rest of his career and incorporated the birds into his still-life studies of the 1870s.

About the Media

Heade painted in brightly colored oils on canvas.

About the Technique

Heade created his paintings from studies and sketches completed on site. He achieved the depth and glowing light of his compositions by applying oil paint in many layers and washes, unifying the color and focusing on atmospheric space. Heade often distorted the perspective of his compositions by elongating form and exaggerating color contrast.

Z. Vanessa Helder
1904-1968

Z. Vanessa Helder (va nes´ ə held´ ər)
was born in Lynden, Washington, where
she began painting when she was only
nine years old. She went to school at the
University of Washington and the Art
Students League in New York, and her
artistic talent was so developed that she was
widely known for her many exhibitions in
New York's art galleries. From 1939 to 1942,
Helder taught watercolor and oil painting
at the Works Progress Administration's Art
Center in Spokane, Washington, and was
very interested in documenting the
construction of the contested Grand
Coulee Dam project.

About Art History

At the time Helder created the Grand Coulee
Dam paintings, America entered World War II,
and publication of her paintings was prohibited
for national security reasons. In 1943, she and
her husband moved to Los Angeles, and during
the same year she exhibited in New York with
other American realists such as Andrew Wyeth,
Peter Blume, and Charles Sheeler.

About the Artwork

Many of Helder's watercolors are landscapes of
the Spokane countryside. Her compositions tended
to be closely cropped so the viewer felt as if the
canvas were brimming with imagery, although her
subject matter did not crowd the work's boundaries.
In *Rocks and Concrete,* the artist's perspective is
level and her forms are lit with daytime light,
allowing the viewer to focus on the color and
texture of the rocks.

About the Media

For a watercolorist, depicting depth and shadows
of forms is a careful process. The artist layers the
paints, using faint washes of color on the paper
and waits for it to dry before applying deeper
tones. Helder used special watercolor paper for
her paintings, which is thick and absorbent, often
with a distinct texture and visible fiber.

About the Technique

Helder traveled to locate subject matter. She would
sketch scenes outdoors and return to her studio to
sketch them again very lightly on paper. It has been
said that she used dinner plates for palettes and
the steering wheel of her car as an easel.

Robert Henri

1865–1929

Robert Henri (rob′ ərt hen′ rē) was born Robert Henry Cozad in Cincinnati, Ohio. He changed his name when his father was accused of murder. Henri showed great artistic talent at a young age and was encouraged by his parents to pursue painting at the Pennsylvania Academy of Fine Arts, and later the Academie Julian and École des Beaux-Arts in Paris, France. When he returned from Paris, he became a widely known and respected teacher, emphasizing the importance of his students' creative freedom. He also stressed his own artistic freedom and founded The Eight, a group of American artists who joined his rebellion against the strict confines of academic art.

About Art History

Henri began his artistic career under the influence of his teacher, Thomas Anshutz, who believed American art should be independent of European domination. After his return from Paris in 1902, Henri taught at the Chase School of Art, the New York School of Art, and the Women's School of Design, where he began his fight against academic art. In 1909, he formed his own art school called *The Eight,* a group comprised of artists who believed art should be relevant to contemporary life. These artists came to be known as the *Ashcan School* and included Arthur B. Davies, William Glackens, Ernest Lawson, George Luks, Maurice Prendergast, Everett Shinn, and John Sloan. As a teacher and an artist Henri believed that people with real talent should be given the opportunity to exhibit, and he worked toward this goal throughout his life.

About the Artwork

The Ashcan School believed that art should apply to everyday life and reflect its reality, not just the popular tastes of the National Academy of Design.

Henri's art embodies this sentiment. He was influenced by the Dutch painter Franz Hals and painted in a realistic manner called *social realism.* His paintings were primarily urban portraits and genre pieces, depicting people's personalities with vitality and spontaneous honesty, as seen in his portrait, *Bernadita.* As a change from painting portraits, Henri sometimes created landscapes, although his true passion was depicting human beings as they really were.

About the Media

Henri's depictions of urban life were created in oils on canvas and his landscapes were created in pastels.

About the Technique

In his classes Henri would promote tonal styles rather than colorist styles, and he painted quickly by slashing thick paint onto his canvas to capture the strength of the moment.

Barbara Hepworth
1903–1975

Barbara Hepworth (bärb´ ə rə hep´ wûrth) was an English sculptor known for her abstract works in wood, stone, and metal. As a child in Yorkshire, she took car trips through the countryside with her father. She was impressed by the contrast between the beauty of rural areas and the grime of industrial towns. The land became a theme she returned to again and again in her art. After studying art and sculpture in England, Hepworth moved to Rome and then returned to England. She married twice, once to a sculptor and once to a painter. She had a son and a set of triplets. Her relationship with her children also became an important theme of her work. In 1965, she was honored by being named a dame of the British Empire.

About Art History

Hepworth's early work was influenced by the sculpture of Jean Arp and Constantin Brancusi, as well as the artwork of her friend Henry Moore. Hepworth and Moore were the most important English sculptors of their time.

About the Artwork

Hepworth was fascinated by relationships. In her sculpture *Mother and Child,* two figures form a single curved shape, indicating their close bond. She expressed her love of nature in such abstract sculptures as *Wave and Tides II.* Hepworth's rounded forms seem to have been shaped by nature instead of a chisel. These sculptures also show her interest in the relationship between the subject and space. She hollowed out forms or pierced them with holes so the space within the sculpture is as important as the sculpture itself. Hepworth often painted the inside surfaces of her sculptures to emphasize the open spaces. She also defined the openings by stretching strings across them. Some of her sculptures are small enough to hold in one hand. Others tower 20 feet above viewers.

About the Media

Hepworth sculpted in wood, stone, marble, alabaster, slate, copper, and bronze.

About the Technique

Hepworth sketched her sculptures before carving them. For her bronze sculptures, she first made plaster models. Her works are notable for their superb finishes.

David Hockney
b. 1937

David Hockney (dā´ vəd häk´ nē) was born in 1937 into a working class family in the northern industrial section of Bradford, England. By the time he was 11, he had decided to become an artist. At 16, he attended the Bradford School of Art, and went on to study at the Royal College of Art. In 1961, he made his first trip to the United States. The brightness and light of California was a sharp contrast from the rain and fog of England. He was impressed by the sense of space in the sprawling city of Los Angeles, and moved permanently to the United States in 1978 to become part of the California art scene.

About Art History

Hockney first made an impact on the art world in the 1960s. He was a leader of the English pop art movement that was centered in London, England. Pop artists were fascinated by how the flood of American mass media was affecting British life. Pop artists used popular or commercial culture as inspiration for their art.

About the Artwork

Hockney is a realistic painter who uses many styles and techniques to tell stories. Much of his artwork relates to his life, family, and friends. Hockney is inspired by the climate and culture of southern California. He is interested in the sunny blue skies and the relaxed lifestyle.

About the Media

Hockney paints with oils and acrylics. He is a stage designer, a printmaker, and a photographer. Hockney creates photo collages that he calls "joiner" photographs. He joins separate photos together to create a unique image that expresses time and movement.

About the Technique

Hockney paints with large areas of bold color. As his style developed he became more interested in how people view his work. He wanted to extend the gaze of his viewers. To create his "joiner" photo collages he alters and combines images to show the passage of time. He may repeat the same image or change the scale or the angle to imply movement. Hockney uses forward and backward progression and organizes all the images to guide the eye to a focal point. He uses an ordinary, automatic 35mm camera and takes a number of pictures in rapid succession.

▲ **Katsushika Hokusai.** (Japanese).
Hokusai as Warrior. c. 1830.

Katsushika Hokusai
1760-1849

Katsushika Hokusai (kät soo´ shē kä hō´ koo sī) was born in the city that is now Tokyo. He changed his name more than 30 times. No one knows why. When his home became dirty, he moved. He lived in 93 different places! Hokusai supported himself by illustrating comic books, greeting cards, and novels. During his lifetime he had two wives and seven children.

Hokusai was not interested in money. To pay his bills he would hand over an envelope of money he had received for a painting. Sometimes it was enough, and sometimes it wasn't. When he was broke, he bought art supplies after dark, hoping to avoid people he owed. Hokusai painted constantly during his later years, barely eating enough to stay alive. He averaged one painting a day, and created 30,000 pieces of art in all.

About Art History

Much of Hokusai's artwork was in a style called *ukiyo-e,* or "floating world." This style focused on nature and people doing everyday things. Hokusai introduced Eastern art to the West. His work strongly influenced other artists such as Manet and Degas.

About the Artwork

Hokusai is best known for his many paintings of Mount Fuji. In some the volcano is framed by an ocean wave. In others, it appears in the background as people go about their daily tasks. Hokusai also painted common Japanese subjects, such as dragons, pagodas, actors, and acrobats.

About the Media

Hokusai was famous for his colored prints on woodblocks. He used a separate block of wood to print each color. He also created oil paintings, ink drawings, and watercolors.

About the Technique

Hokusai was a master of brush painting. He used a brush with a tip that was round and pointed instead of flat. Brush painting can show both hard outlines and soft strokes. As Hokusai grew older, his brushstrokes became softer and less controlled. He began to use transparent washes of colors rather than opaque paint.

Allan Houser
1915-1994

Born in Oklahoma, Allan Houser (a´ lən hou´ zər) was the great-nephew of the Apache chief Geronimo. In 1929, he left high school to help out on his family's farm, but he was also able to study his passion—art. In 1936, his paintings were shown at the World's Fair in New York. After he painted several large murals for government buildings in Washington, D.C. in 1939 and 1940, he began to explore sculpture. Houser made small wood carvings while he taught art and worked as a pipe fitter's assistant.

About Art History

Houser taught at many schools including 13 years at the Institute of American Indian Arts at the Santa Fe Indian School. As a teacher, he influenced nearly every modern Native American sculptor. With work ranging from realistic to abstract, Houser used art to teach others about Native Americans and to express his pride in his heritage.

About the Artwork

Most of Houser's subjects were related to his background. Examples include *Offering of the Sacred Pipe, The Future Chircahua Apache Family,* and a bronze bust of Geronimo. Houser also illustrated books about Native Americans.

About the Media

Houser created sculpture in stone, steel, and bronze. In addition to painting in oils, watercolors, acrylics, and egg tempera, he worked in charcoals and pastels.

About the Technique

Houser urged his students to search for what satisfied them. He said, "I first please myself. If I don't please myself, no one else will be pleased."

Mary Jackson
b. 1945

Mary Jackson (mâ´ rē jak´ sən) was born in South Carolina and learned how to make baskets from her mother when she was four years old. After graduating from high school, Jackson stopped making baskets and moved to New York. She resumed making baskets in her spare time when she moved back to the south in 1972. When Jackson left her secretarial job to be at home with her son she began making baskets full time. She believes this art form puts her in touch with her ancestors and history. Jackson travels across the country to present lectures on her cultural heritage at museums, galleries, and conventions. She also leads workshops in schools and arts organizations throughout the United States.

About Art History

Jackson's ancestors brought the tradition of basket making with them to America. Men and boys gathered the materials, and women and girls constructed the baskets. The baskets were used to carry rice grains on plantations, and plantation owners valued the experienced basket makers for their skills. This attention caused the basket makers to become secretive about their techniques so outsiders wouldn't exploit their talent into a commercial commodity. Today basket-making skills are passed down from generation to generation.

About the Artwork

Jackson has introduced new modern shapes and designs to traditional basket making, though she continues to study traditional methods. Patterning is often important in her works and many are made with multiple types of grass with light and dark colors. In addition to being works of art, these baskets can also serve as bread baskets or storage containers.

About the Media

Sweetgrass can only be found in the coastal dunes of the southeastern United States. Increased coastal development in the region is quickly consuming wetlands, the natural habitat for sweetgrass. Artists like Jackson hope a material shortage will not erase the tradition of basket making. Sometimes Jackson adds other natural materials such as pine needles or palmetto fibers for accents and coiling in her baskets.

About the Technique

It takes a long time to create sweetgrass baskets, and some of the larger, more detailed pieces take months to make. Sweetgrass is harvested by hand from the wetlands of South Carolina and then dried in the sun. It is then woven with palmetto fronds into row upon row of coiled grass. The coils are continually fed with new grasses to maintain a uniform thickness and then stitched together with dried strips of palm leaf. The strength of the basket depends on how tightly the stitches are pulled.

Joshua Johnson
active 1796–1824

▲ **Joshua Johnson.** (American).
The Westwood Children. c. 1807.

Oil on canvas. 41 1/8 × 46 inches (104.5 x 116.8 cm.).
National Gallery of Art, Washington, D.C.

Born into slavery in Baltimore, Maryland, Joshua Johnson (jäsh´ wə jän´ sən) received his freedom in 1782 and advertised himself as a portrait painter in Baltimore, becoming the first successful African American portraitist. Johnson moved around Baltimore frequently, and it is thought that he may have supplemented his career by painting furniture. Little is known of his later life and activities, and no recorded information exists concerning his whereabouts or career after 1824.

About Art History

Specific influences on Johnson's painting and his training are unknown, although his work exhibits similarities to that of other painters at the time, such as Charles Peale Polk and Ralph Earl. He is thought to have been self taught and financially supported by the portrait commissions of wealthy Baltimore patrons. Some have speculated that he was at one time a blacksmith.

About the Artwork

Johnson painted his portraits in a conventional English style, usually representing his subjects with stiff arms, hands, and legs, and facial expressions. His paintings were typically *busts*, focusing on the head and shoulders of subjects, and depicting them in a three-quarters pose with slightly upturned eyes and pressed lips. The figures are painted on a dark, somber background and often hold objects such as a pencil, basket, parasol, book, or riding crop.

Johnson's group portrait, *The Westwood Children*, employs these qualities, as we see the children portrayed with serious gazes and little emotion. This composition is painted with Johnson's harsh linear style and two-dimensional depth.

About the Media

Johnson's oil paintings were typically portraits of wealthy merchants and their families. He rarely signed his paintings, so the total number of his works is unknown, although about eighty compositions have been attributed to him.

About the Technique

Many of Johnson's stern portraits were painted with sparse amounts of paint. Most portraits at that time were created from live models, and Johnson probably sketched and painted portraits of his subjects as they sat before him.

William Johnson

Little is known about the artist who created this watercolor love token aside from his name. It is assumed that William Johnson made this piece while living in Pennsylvania, and that he may have been of German or English heritage. The style of the artwork as well as the location where its owner lived suggests that it was made by a member of the extensive Pennsylvania German community during the early nineteenth century.

◀ **William Johnson.** (American).
Lovebird Token. Early nineteenth century.

Watercolor and ink on cut paper. $16\frac{1}{8} \times 16$ inches (41 × 40.6 cm.).
American Folk Art Museum, New York, New York.

About Art History

During the early years of American history, love tokens were exchanged between young men and women on February fourteenth, also known as Valentine's Day. Love tokens were affectionate poems or verses written onto various kinds of paper artwork, such as paintings, geometric-patterned foldings or cuttings, woven paper strips, lace design paper cutouts, or even simple drawings. Although the exact origin of American love tokens is not known, some of the imagery seen on these tokens appears to be from British or Germanic cultures. For example, the interlaced knot design dates back to medieval European designs symbolic of never-ending love. Similar forms of interlaced artwork have been seen in medieval Germanic decorative art.

About the Artwork

The *Lovebird Token* has a beautiful geometric design made of concentric rings and a detailed central illustration. Each of the rings displays lines of a poem dedicated to the recipient of the love token, an unnamed young woman.

About the Media

The *Lovebird Token* was painted in watercolors and ink on cut paper.

About the Technique

The round cut-work of this *Lovebird Token* is an example of a popular style of love token made in many of the Pennsylvania German communities of the nineteenth century. The bright colors and images of kissing birds were also common features of love tokens from this time period.

Wassily Kandinsky

1866-1944

Wassily Kandinsky (va sēl´ ē kan din´ skē) first tried painting as a teenager in his native Russia. Even then he felt that each color had a mysterious life of its own. He was still drawn to colors and painting while he studied law and economics in college, but he believed that art was "a luxury forbidden to a Russian." In time, he moved to Germany, studied art, and began his career. Throughout his life Kandinsky moved back and forth between Russia and Germany. In 1933 he settled in France after Nazi storm troopers labeled his painting style "degenerate."

About Art History

Kandinsky was a pioneer in the pure abstract painting style—a combination of color and form with no subject matter. He did not give a title to a painting he did in 1910, but others called it the *First Abstract Watercolour.* Kandinsky felt that trying to paint recognizable objects distracted artists from their real jobs of expressing ideas and emotions. He believed communicating through painting was similar to communicating with music. He often gave his paintings titles that were musical and abstract, such as *Improvisation 30.*

About the Artwork

It is possible to identify landscapes and objects in some of Kandinsky's early paintings, but his later work was entirely abstract. Only occasionally during World War I did Kandinsky include cannons and other recognizable objects in his work.

About the Media

Kandinsky worked in oils, watercolors, and India ink.

About the Technique

Kandinsky did not try to show the essence of his subjects because he had none. Instead, he attempted to make forms and colors take on meaning separate from the physical world. His work often impresses even viewers who are not certain what the paintings mean.

Paul Klee
1879–1940

Paul Klee (paul klā) was born into a musical Swiss family. His family hoped he also would become a musician. At age five his grandmother gave him his first box of pencils. He thought of himself as an artist from then on, but he continued to have an interest in music. Klee played his violin for an hour nearly every morning of his life. He married a pianist. As an adult Klee still drew in a childlike way. Klee believed that childlike drawings were the most creative and original. He was not trying to share his ideas through his work. He just wanted to explore his imagination. Klee could use either hand proficiently when painting.

About Art History

At first, art critics ignored Klee's work. Then they realized that his small, charming, playful pictures were filled with ideas and meaning. Different people find different meanings in Klee's pictures. For many people this adds to the value of his work.

About the Artwork

Klee studied nature and often began his paintings with an image from nature. Then he would let his imagination take over.

About the Media

Klee painted with watercolors and other materials on paper, canvas, silk, linen, and burlap. He liked to experiment; for example, he did one picture with black paste on burlap.

About the Technique

Color was important to Klee. He once said, "Color and I are one; I am a painter." In his watercolors Klee used thin layers of pale color. This technique made his pictures gently shimmer like pavement under a hot sun. Klee used color the way a musician uses sound. He tried to touch the feelings of his viewers. Klee said that he learned more about painting from the musicians Bach and Mozart than he did from other visual artists.

Lee Krasner
1908–1984

Lee Krasner (lē kraz´ nər) was a major figure in the first generation of American artists. She developed a new style of abstract painting in the late 1940s and early 1950s. As the wife of Jackson Pollock, the acknowledged leader of abstract expressionism, Krasner participated in the style's evolution. She was known for bringing color back into the all-over technique that she and Pollock shared. During much of her lifetime Krasner's reputation was obscured by her husband's accomplishments.

About Art History

In the years just after World War II, the United States became a global power and American artists practicing a new style known as *abstract expressionism* emerged as leaders in the art world. For the first time Western Europeans began to look to New York for artistic direction. Abstract expressionism uses a nonrepresentational approach to color and form in order to express emotions.

About the Artwork

Because of its abstraction, Krasner's work invites the emotional and intuitive interpretation of viewers. The artist's physical experience of creating the painting becomes a metaphor for life itself.

About the Media

Krasner applied large amounts of oil paint to unprimed canvases. She used commercial painters' brushes, a palette knife, and sticks, among other tools.

About the Technique

Krasner poured and dripped paint over the entire surface of the canvas to create a network of interwoven colors. Krasner worked from right to left in most of her paintings. Curves, dots, and dashes were also dabbed on straight from the paint tube. The intensity of color in Krasner's paintings reflects the artist's creative energy.

Jacob Lawrence

1917–2000

Jacob Lawrence (jā´ kəb lär´ ənz) had parents who met on their migration to the North. His father was born in South Carolina, and his mother in Virginia. Lawrence was born in Atlantic City, New Jersey, in 1917. The family finally settled in Harlem in 1929 at the end of the Harlem Renaissance. Because his mother worked all day, she enrolled Lawrence in the Harlem Art Workshop after school to keep him out of trouble. He had many excellent teachers there, including Charles Alston. Lawrence won a scholarship to the American Artists School. He taught at New York's Pratt Institute from 1958 to 1965. From 1970, he taught at the University of Washington in Seattle, where he also served as head of the art department. He won many awards in his lifetime, including the Presidential Medal of Arts.

About Art History

Lawrence's paintings not only contribute to the art world, they also add to our knowledge of African American history. Lawrence painted African American heroes, such as Harriet Tubman and Frederick Douglass.

About the Artwork

Lawrence's most famous work is a series of 60 paintings called *Migration of the Negro.* The paintings tell a story which begins at a train station in the South and ends at a station in the North. The scenes he chose to paint focus on the struggle of leaving one life for another and the search for freedom and dignity. His paintings did not overlook the harshness and violence that was part of this migration. During World War II he served in the U.S. Coast Guard and created a series of paintings about his experiences. They were exhibited by the Museum of Modern Art in 1944.

About the Media

Lawrence painted on paper with *gouache,* an opaque watercolor paint, similar to tempera paint used in schools. It covers the paper with a smooth, matte coat. He was also a printmaker.

About the Technique

Lawrence said a lot about his subjects with only a few lines and carefully chosen colors. He used many neutral colors, such as taupe, mocha, and charcoal, and balanced them with splashes of bright color.

Judith Leyster
1609-1660

Judith Leyster (jo͞o´ dəth lā´ stər) was an artist who excelled at painting the familiar— ordinary people pursuing daily activities. Leyster was licensed in 1633 as a painter in the Guild of St. Luke of Haarlem in the Netherlands. Most of her signed and dated paintings were made before her 1636 marriage to another genre painter, Jan Miense Molenaer. It seems she stopped painting after she married. Leyster often signed her work with a distinctive monogram, her initials intertwined with a star. This signature was intended as a pun on the artist's name that means "leading star."

▲ **Judith Leyster.** (Dutch). *Self-Portrait.* c. 1630.
. . . .
Oil on canvas. $29\frac{3}{8} \times 25\frac{7}{8}$ inches (73.66 × 65.72 cm.).
National Gallery of Art, Washington, D.C.

About Art History

Genre painting—painting scenes of everyday life— was popular in the Netherlands during the seventeenth century. The country's prosperous merchants were eager to buy portraits, landscapes, still lifes, and genre paintings for their homes. Scenes of merrymaking, such as *The Concert,* were popular. Leyster's style shows the influence of other Haarlem artists such as Frans Hals and Frans de Grebber, who may have been her teachers.

About the Artwork

In *The Concert* a trio of musicians—a violinist, a lute player, and a singer—are playing in an unspecified setting. Two look out at the viewer, while the woman looks upward, enraptured by the joy of music-making. Symbolically this painting expresses the virtue of harmony. The singer, counting out time with her hand, looks like the artist herself. The violin player is thought to be her husband. While they are dressed in fashionable Dutch attire—dark clothing with broad lace collars—the lute player has put a festive red costume over his more somber, everyday clothing.

About the Media

Leyster applied oil paint to canvas. In other works she painted on a wood panel.

About the Technique

Leyster favored creating an intimate composition with a single figure or a small group of figures in an interior setting. In this work the musicians are close to the picture plane; the space they inhabit joins that of the viewer. The brilliantly illuminated faces, the white collars, and the red costume of the lute player stand out against the dark background.

Jacques Lipchitz
1891–1973

Jacques Lipchitz (zhäk lēp´shēts) was born in Lithuania and later moved to France. During World War II Lipchitz, who was Jewish, fled Europe to escape the Nazis. He left Paris and came to the United States. In 1952 a fire destroyed everything in his New York art studio, and he had to start all over. In 1957 he became a citizen of the United States.

About Art History

By the 1930s, Lipchitz was known as one of the leading European sculptors. After meeting the Spanish artist Picasso, Lipchitz was influenced by the cubist style. Both expressionism and surrealism influenced his work. Many of Lipchitz's works had political themes. For example, Lipchitz believed it was important to speak out against Nazism in his work. He tried to convey the idea that to create freely, one must fight evil.

About the Artwork

Lipchitz's work reflects many different styles and themes. Some are realistic, while others are abstract. Some sculptures were planned in detail, and others were made quickly, without much planning. Lipchitz became known for bronze sculptures that he called *transparencies.* These sculptures include solid areas and holes. Lipchitz often used biblical and mythological stories to express his anger about Nazism. For example, he showed David and Goliath with the giant wearing a swastika, the emblem of Nazi Germany.

About the Media

Lipchitz created bronze and stone sculptures as well as wooden panels.

About the Technique

Lipchitz sketched an idea first. Then he made a small model from plaster or wax. Using the model as a guide, Lipchitz would cast a larger sculpture out of bronze or carve it out of stone.

Henri Matisse
1869-1954

Henri Matisse (än´ rē ma tēs´) was the son of a middle-class couple in the north of France. He was not interested in art while he was in school. After high school his father sent him to law school in Paris. When he was 21 an appendicitis attack changed his life. Because he had to spend a long time in the hospital, his mother brought him a paint box to help him pass the time. Matisse eventually convinced his father to let him drop out of law school and study art. Matisse married and started a family soon after. His paintings were not selling, so he worked for a decorator and his wife opened a hat shop. During the last years of his life he suffered from arthritis. Unable to hold a brush in his hands, he devoted his efforts to making paper cutouts from papers painted to his specifications, and he created fantastic, brightly colored shapes. Unlike many other artists, he was internationally famous during his lifetime.

About Art History

In 1905, Matisse and his friends exhibited a painting style that showed strong emotionalism, wild colors, and distortion of shape. They were called *les fauves,* or "the wild beasts," and they experimented with intense, sometimes violent colors. Without letting their work become abstract, Matisse and other fauvist painters tested the bounds of reality.

About the Artwork

Matisse painted still lifes, room interiors, and landscapes. His paintings of dancers and human figures were generally more concerned with expressive shapes than an accurate representation of anatomy.

About the Media

Matisse painted primarily with oils, and also created many prints. Later in life he worked with cut paper.

About the Technique

Matisse worked with bold, intense colors. He simplified and distorted shapes for expressive qualities. He was most interested in the way visual elements were organized.

Carolyn Mazloomi
b. 1948

Fiber artist, author, lecturer, and historian Carolyn Mazloomi (ka´ rə lin maz lōō´ mē) is considered one of America's leading quilters and is recognized for founding the Women of Color Quilters' Network, an international organization that promotes the fiber art creations of African Americans. Mazloomi is also the author of *Spirits of the Cloth,* a book celebrating the quilts and stories of contemporary African American fiber artists. Her work has been exhibited across the United States and internationally, and her book *Spirits of the Cloth* earned the Best Nonfiction Book of the Year award from the American Library Association.

About Art History

African American quilting is a tradition dating back to colonial times. These quilts are highly valued today because they vibrantly express a wide range of creativity and technique. Each quilt is different, reflecting diverse images of memory, social and political issues, poetry, jazz, personal experience, or narrative.

About the Artwork

Mazloomi had not quilted before she attended an art show that displayed Appalachian quilts. In fact, with a doctorate in aerospace engineering, she began a career working in airplane research before she saw her first quilt. She was so inspired by its simple beauty that she decided to teach herself how to create them. Mazloomi's quilts refer to African American life and history, as well as a shared African ancestry. She uses bright colors and actively patterned figures in many of her quilts. At times she also incorporates masks into her work, as seen in her piece *Mask Communion.*

About the Media

Mazloomi's quilts are made from different fabrics from around the world. The vibrant colors in her quilts include deep reds and purples, and bright oranges and blues; sometimes her quilts are created solely with black and white fabrics.

About the Technique

Mazloomi uses piecing, appliqué, painting, stamping, and quilting to form her quilts. She cuts out her shapes freehand and fits them together onto backgrounds with colorful needlework. When she begins to create a piece, she does not have an image of the finished product in mind. Instead she works improvisationally.

Gu Mei

1619–1664

Gu Mei (gŌŌ mā) was born in Nanjing, China. She held a unique place among the intellectuals of the time because she was not only a talented musician and poet, but also a painter. Gu Mei married a respected poet, Gong Dingzi.

▲ **Gu Mei.** (Chinese). *Orchids and Rocks.* 1644. Ming Dynasty.

Detail of handscroll ink on paper. $10\frac{5}{8} \times 67\frac{1}{4}$ inches (27 × 170.8 cm.). Arthur M. Sackler Gallery, Smithsonian Institution, Washington, D.C.

About Art History

After the Mongol overlords of the previous dynasty were defeated, the Ming Dynasty began. It was the last dynasty of native rule. Great artists of the time were said to possess *qi,* or "divine spirit," which allowed them to paint the truth beneath the surface. A famous critic and artist of the Ming Dynasty, Dong Qichang, praised artists who could paint in a way that transformed the old styles. Gu Mei lived during a time of great artistic freedom.

About the Artwork

Paintings of the human body were given the highest status in Europe, but in China it was landscape drawings that were most valued. Gu Mei often drew landscapes and orchids.

About the Media

Like other artists of her time, Gu Mei painted with ink on paper or silk scrolls.

About the Technique

Gu Mei combined delicate brushwork with fluid motions when creating her paintings.

Michelangelo
1475-1564

Michelangelo (mī kə lan´ jə lō) Buonarroti was born in the mountain village of Caprese, Italy. Even at an early age, his talent for drawing was obvious. His father, a Florentine official who was connected to the ruling Medici family, apprenticed his son to the master painter Ghirlandaio. After two years Michelangelo attended the sculpture school sponsored by the Medici family. He was introduced to the leaders of France by Lorenzo de´ Medici. When Lorenzo died, Michelangelo fled to Rome, where he examined many newly unearthed classical statues. In 1505, he was given two commissions: a tomb for Julius II, and the painting of the ceiling of the Sistine Chapel. It took him four years to cover the ceiling with fresco painting. He completed the Sistine Chapel by covering the altar wall with a fresco, *The Last Judgment.*

▲ **Marcello Venusti.** (Italian).
Portrait of Michelangelo. 1535.

Casa Buonarroti, Florence, Italy.

About Art History

Michelangelo was one of the most inspired creators in the history of art, and along with Leonardo da Vinci, one of the leading forces in the Italian High Renaissance. He was a sculptor, architect, and painter. He had a tremendous influence on his contemporaries and on the western European art that followed.

About the Artwork

Like other artists of his time, Michelangelo focused on religious topics. Among his timeless works of art are the ceiling of the Sistine Chapel, the statue of *David,* his painting *The Last Judgment,* and the design of St. Peter's Basilica.

About the Media

Michelangelo carved magnificent marble statues. He painted using a fresco technique that requires working with plaster, pigments, and water.

About the Technique

To create his sculptures, Michelangelo carved directly into marble using chisels and finishing tools after much careful planning. For a fresco painting, he first drew a "cartoon" and transferred the image to a wall or ceiling before he began painting. Plaster was applied only to the area that would be painted that day. Pigment was mixed with water and applied directly to the wet plaster. The color would then become part of the plaster, remaining as bright as when it was applied.

Joan Miró
1893–1983

Joan Miró (hō´ än mē rō´) entered art school in his native Spain when he was a teenager. His teachers introduced him to modern art, but in time he developed his own style, moving from traditional painting to surreal fantasy. Miró lived in Spain and France and focused entirely on his art. By the end of World War II he was very famous. He painted a wall-sized mural for Harvard University, and created two ceramic walls for the UNESCO building in Paris, France. Both the cities of Houston, Texas, and Chicago, Illinois, asked him to create huge sculptures. Miró received numerous awards for his artwork. He lived a quiet life, and although his work received much attention, Miró remained in the background. Creating art was his whole life.

About Art History

Miró was fascinated with symbols. He wanted to show nature as it would be painted by a primitive artist or a child. He was influenced by the dadaists, the surrealists, and Paul Klee's childlike drawings. Miró also encouraged many young artists—especially in the United States—to experiment and move away from realism.

About the Artwork

Miró began by painting landscapes, portraits, and still lifes. Later he moved on to create "dream pictures" and imaginary landscapes. In these, Miró showed his view of harsh modern life. Some of the shapes he painted look like amoeba or graffiti. Miró's work became simpler as he grew older. For example, one of his later paintings, *Blue II,* consists of several dots and an orange line on a blue surface.

About the Media

Miró expressed his fantasies through a wide variety of media. He created drawings, paintings, collages, lithographs, murals, tapestries, sculptures, and ceramic pieces. He even designed costumes and settings for the play *Romeo and Juliet.*

Henry Moore
1898–1986

Henry Moore (hen´ rē mor) was born in Castleford, England. When he was ten, he told his father he wanted to become a sculptor. At 18, he left home to join the army during World War I. He began studying art after the war. By age 23, he was a serious sculptor.

About Art History

In the 1930s, many sculptors were producing realistic works. However, Moore and a few of his artist friends started creating sculpture that was more abstract. Moore simplified human figures and emphasized carving forms. He used holes in his sculptures, which he associated with the mystery of caves. His early works show the influence of Mexican and African carvings. Many critics consider Moore the greatest English sculptor of the 1900s.

About the Artwork

Moore frequently combined his figures with shapes and textures from nature. He focused on making the simplest form of the subject he carved. Moore thought of his large sculptures as part of the open air with the sky as the background. Families were an important subject of his sculptures. His own family inspired his work.

About the Media

Moore carved some sculptures in wood and some in stone. Most of his large sculptures were cast in bronze.

About the Technique

Moore collected pebbles, flint rocks, shells, animal bones, and old, weathered pieces of wood for his studio. These pieces inspired him to draw. From his sketches, he made small models for his sculptures, then he made larger models. After much planning he was ready to make the actual sculptures.

Giorgio Morandi
1890–1964

Giorgio Morandi (jor´ jē ō mo rän´ dē) was born in Bologna, Italy, and became one of the most respected masters in modern Italian art. After displaying an artistic talent at a very young age, Morandi in 1907 enrolled in the Academy of Fine Arts in Bologna. His scholastic performance was excellent at first, but conflicts arose with his professors when his changing interests led him to develop his own artistic language. Morandi began to exhibit his work in 1914 and taught for many years in the municipally-run drawing schools. After World War II broke out in 1943, he moved to Grizzana and began producing exceptional still lifes and landscapes. Morandi continued to paint until he died in Bologna after a year-long illness.

▲ **Giorgio Morandi.** (Italian). *Self-Portrait.* 1924.

Pinacoteca di Brera, Milan, Italy.

About Art History

After receiving his diploma, Morandi collected black and white reproductions of paintings, particularly those of Cézanne and Rousseau. In 1930, he was elected the chair of engraving at the Academy of Fine Arts, where he taught until 1956. Morandi exhibited his work in the most exclusive international circles, especially in northern Europe and in the United States.

About the Artwork

Morandi began with a metaphysical painting style, an important step leading up to surrealism in the late 1910s. By the time he reached his twenties, he rejected that movement and created his own style based on his internalized vision. His still lifes and landscapes were sophisticated and poetic, and his compositions of bottles, jugs, and bowls were emphasized by their rich colors. Morandi also created brilliant etchings and was famous for his clever use of light within these etchings.

About the Media

Morandi created drawings, etchings, and prints, and therefore used a variety of media, such as pen and black ink, watercolors, acrylics, and pastels on paper.

About the Technique

In 1914 Morandi began teaching himself to etch using old manuals, and etching continued to be important to him throughout his career. He created still lifes with groupings of enigmatic objects but later pursued a more formal style.

Berthe Morisot
1841–1865

Berthe Morisot (bârt môr ē´ s ō) was born in France. She was the granddaughter of the painter Fragonard. Taught by her father, she learned how to draw when she was very young. Later she took painting lessons with her sister. She began selling her paintings when she was 23, but she never felt that she was treated as an equal of male painters. When she was 33, she married Eugene Manet, the brother of Édouard Manet. They had one daughter, Julie.

About Art History

Morisot was a pupil of the French realist painter Corot, but she was influenced primarily by Édouard Manet. She regularly exhibited with the impressionists, against the advice of her family and friends. These painters were interested in how light looked when it reflected off of objects. They often painted landscapes in light pastel colors like yellow, blue, and green. Morisot was friends with many artists, including Degas, who painted in the impressionist style. Morisot and Cassat are often considered the most important female painters of the nineteenth century. Édouard Manet was convinced by Morisot to change his palette and to abandon black.

About the Artwork

Morisot painted genre paintings of women in their homes wearing expensive dresses and hats. She also liked to paint images of people in gardens of trees, flowers, and bushes. She took advantage of how light played off these surfaces.

About the Media

Morisot generally painted in oil on canvas. She also made some paintings with watercolors, pastels, and hard steel pencils on paper.

About the Technique

Morisot made her paintings seem light and soft by working quickly. Her work looks like it is done with swift, sketchy strokes. Few contours or details were used. When she painted, she put a lot of paint on her brush, but she hardly touched the canvas. Sometimes she drew a scene in pencil first, and then painted patches of bright colors across the surface.

Elizabeth Murray
b. 1940

Elizabeth Murray (ē li´ zə bəth mûr´ ē) was born in Chicago, Illinois. Her artistic abilities were evident during elementary school when she sold drawings of elephants, cowboys, and stagecoaches to her classmates for 25 cents apiece. Murray attended the Art Institute of Chicago, where she took classes in figure drawing, landscape painting, and traditional techniques. She attended Mills College in Oakland, California and moved to New York City in 1967. Her first solo exhibition was held in 1976, and now her paintings and prints are found in major collections throughout the United States.

About Art History

At the Art Institute of Chicago, Murray studied paintings by artists with a variety of styles, including Cézanne, Seurat, and Willem de Kooning. Her use of color resembles that of Matisse and Cézanne. Her whimsical portrayal of everyday objects is influenced by styles from impressionism to expressionism. Murray's contemporaries are minimalists, but her work more closely resembles abstract and pop art paintings.

About the Artwork

Murray is always trying to devise a new way of painting and redefining structure. She developed a style that combines painting and sculpture and is now considered a master of the shaped canvas. She often creates works of art that display domestic objects in a state of disarray. She was interested in comics early in her career, as well as three-dimensional painting elements. Murray overlapped shaped canvases to create a small amount of depth in *Riverbank,* a nonobjective work that implies the outdoors through colors and shapes.

About the Media

Murray uses oils on canvas.

About the Technique

Murray layers shaped canvases to create depth. She also layers the paint in thick strokes to extend this feeling of depth. Each painting begins as a small drawing, and then becomes a clay model. Finally Murray covers formed sheets of plywood with canvas and begins to paint.

Michael Naranjo

b. 1944

Michael Naranjo (mī´ kəl nä rän´ hō) was born into a family of artists in the Tewa Indian pueblo in Santa Clara, New Mexico. His mother and three of his nine brothers and sisters are artists or writers. Naranjo's mother, a ceramic artist, taught all of her children to sculpt in clay. As a child Naranjo liked to make models of animals and people using his mother's clay.

In 1967 Naranjo was drafted into the army and sent to fight in the Vietnam War. When he was only 22 years old, a grenade exploded near his face, and he lost his eyesight. His right hand was also severely injured. Despite these disabilities, he used his skills to create figures in wax, and in 1969 his first show of small figurines was held in the VA medical center in Albuquerque, New Mexico. He has been allowed to touch many artworks, including *David* in Florence, Italy, and *Venus de Milo* at the Louvre in Paris, France. Naranjo married a nurse and has two daughters.

About Art History

Naranjo uses his skills to celebrate his culture while helping others learn about Native American traditions and ceremonies. Naranjo also spends much of his time making artwork accessible to the blind. He has organized a touchable art exhibition at the Heard Museum in Phoenix, Arizona, and also established the Touched by Art Fund to provide students with financing so they are able to visit museums. He was named the Outstanding Disabled Veteran of the Year in 1999.

About the Artwork

Naranjo often sculpts Native American dancers. His intense *Taos Hoop Dancer* is less than a foot high, while his impressive *War Dancer* is 12 feet tall. Naranjo also sculpts animals and people in the outdoors. He often uses dark clay, or bronze with a dark patina, symbolic of his blindness.

About the Media

Naranjo models his sculptures in wax or clay. His bronze works are cast at a foundry.

About the Technique

Naranjo sometimes thinks about a sculpture for weeks, or even years, before he creates it. Sometimes he uses a model before he begins, memorizing the contours that he will create in the final work. He usually uses his hands to sculpt because he is not able to feel the ends of tools. He adds the etching and final details with his fingernails. Naranjo tries to eliminate all unnecessary details in his work, shaping only the pure form that is in his mind's eye.

Georgia O'Keeffe
1887–1986

Georgia O'Keeffe (jôr′ jə ō kēf′) was born in Sun Prairie, Wisconsin. At the age of ten she began taking private art lessons, but the thing she liked most was experimenting with art at home. By 13, she had decided to become an artist. She trained under experts and won many prizes for her art. For years she challenged the art world with her unique vision. She eventually became famous for her spectacular, larger-than-life paintings of natural objects, including flowers, animal skulls, and shells. She loved nature, especially the desert of New Mexico, where she spent the last half of her life. O'Keeffe was married to the famous American photographer Alfred Stieglitz and appears in many of his photographs. In 1997, a Georgia O'Keeffe Museum opened in Santa Fe, New Mexico. It is the first museum in the United States devoted exclusively to the work of a major female artist.

About Art History

Stieglitz promoted modern artists and photographers from Europe and America through a magazine called *Camera Work* and a gallery known as "291." O'Keeffe and the circle of artists she met through Stieglitz were pioneers of modernism in the United States. She took subjects into her imagination and altered and simplified their appearances. She expressed her emotions through her vivid paintings.

About the Artwork

O'Keeffe's artwork features bold, colorful, abstract patterns and shapes. She most often painted natural forms such as flowers and bleached bones, pulling them out of their usual environments. She never painted portraits but sometimes painted landscapes.

About the Media

O'Keeffe used oils and watercolors for her paintings. She used pastels, charcoal, and pencil for her drawings.

About the Technique

O'Keeffe worked in dazzling, jewel-toned colors. She chose unusual perspectives, such as very close up or far away. She also enlarged the scale of her subjects.

Clara Peeters
1594–1657

Clara Peeters (klä´ ra pē´ tərz), who lived in Antwerp, Flanders (Belgium), was one of the originators of still-life painting in the seventeenth century. She produced, signed, and dated paintings while she was a teenager. Very little is known about her education, her life, and her career.

◀ **Clara Peeters.** (Belgian). *Portrait of a lady believed to be Clara Peeters* (detail). 17ᵗʰ century.

Oil on panel. Phillips' Fine Art Auctioneers, London England.

About Art History

During the seventeenth century, new types of subject matter entered the art world, especially in northern Europe. Among them were *still lifes*—arrangements of both natural objects such as fruits and flowers, and human-made objects. Numerous categories of still-life paintings evolved. Peeters is associated with those known as the *breakfast piece,* which depicts a light meal eaten at any time of day, and the *banquet piece,* a luxurious display of food, drink, and table settings. Many women established successful careers painting still lifes.

About the Artwork

In *Still Life of Fish and Cat,* a cat intrudes on this tempting array of exotic seafood which includes bass, oyster, eel, and shrimp. Peeters convincingly rendered the textures of the seafood and the containers. Typical of the time period, the arrangement is placed against a dark background on a shallow shelf; tendrils of the shrimp trail over its edge. Although the work is not dated, it was most likely produced after 1620, when the artist's style changed from more elaborate arrangements to simpler compositions with fewer objects and monochromatic color schemes.

About the Media

Peeters used oil paints on panels, a common medium for artists working in northern Europe at this time.

About the Technique

Peeters demonstrated her technical virtuosity in the reflection of the shrimp on the polished metal plate. The brown color scheme creates visual interest through the contrasting textures of the fish scales, oyster shell, cat fur, and ceramic.

▲ French School. (France). *Camille Pissarro.*
....
Photograph. Musee Marmottan, Paris, France.

Camille Pissarro
1830–1903

Camille Pissarro (kä mēl´ pə sär´ ō) was born in the Virgin Islands. As a young boy, he attended boarding school near Paris. Although his father was a prosperous merchant, Pissarro was not interested in following the family business, so at the age of 25 he went to live and paint in Paris. He was regarded by his contemporaries as a virtuous man—loyal, patient, honest, and wise with his friends and his family. He was revered by younger painters such as Degas and Cézanne, and was considered the unofficial moderator among the earlier group of impressionists. Although he endured financial hardship throughout his career, by the age of 62 he finally established a sound reputation and actively painted until he died in Paris at the age of 73.

About Art History

Along with Claude Monet and others, Pissarro was an original member of the impressionist movement. For Pissarro, Monet, and others such as Degas, Cézanne, and Gauguin, this "impression" was very important, as they abandoned the strict attention to form and paid greater attention to the manner and effect of light in their subjects. Though some of the impressionists eventually began painting in a highly abstract manner, Pissarro maintained the relative discipline of early impressionism by balancing his exploration of light with a respect for the material form of his subjects.

About the Artwork

Outdoor light and atmosphere were the main elements studied by the early impressionists, and Pissarro's work reflects this study. He explored the vivacious quality of cityscapes, as in *The Market at Gisors*. He also depicted the simple, yet noble character of natural landscapes, as in *Landscape*

with Fields. Pissarro emphasized the arrangement of space and well-defined contours among the abstract details of his paintings. He was the first of the impressionists to use divided colors in his brushstrokes.

About the Media

Pissarro painted primarily with oil paints, although some of his works were done in pastels. He was also very talented at drawing, and many of his days as a young artist were spent drawing the port in his hometown of St. Thomas.

About the Technique

Pissarro applied his paint in a series of scattered dots and comma brushstrokes, which simplified the form of his subjects and focused on the activity of light. These small swatches of color work together to reflect a sense of his subject's actual form, and they depict a conscious carefulness.

Richard Pousette-Dart

1916–1992

Richard Pousette-Dart (ri shâr´ pū set´ där) was born in Minnesota. His parents encouraged his interest in the arts. His father was an artist and writer, and his mother was a poet and musician. His family moved near New York City when he was two. Pousette-Dart dropped out of college to live in New York City. He worked as a secretary during the day and painted only at night, struggling for recognition. After he became successful he moved to a rural area so he could work alone. In 1959 he returned to the city to teach other artists to use self-discovery in their works. Pousette-Dart married a poet, and they had two children.

About Art History

At one time Pousette-Dart was the youngest of the New York abstract expressionists, but he led the others in experimenting with different art forms. A thoughtful man, Pousette-Dart used both art and poetry to express his ideas. He believed that art should be appreciated for the quality of the work, not because of the artist who created it; thus, he rarely signed his work.

About the Artwork

Pousette-Dart's first paintings were abstract but could be recognized as birds, fish, and snails. He quickly moved to totally abstract art. Many of his early paintings consist of whirling forms that suggest motion and life. Later he began to use lines and dots to suggest stillness.

About the Media

Pousette-Dart painted with oils, watercolors, and acrylics. He also experimented with sculpture and collage. For these works, he used brass, stone, wire, clay, plaster, sand, and found objects such as bottle caps.

About the Technique

Pousette-Dart did not plan or sketch his work. Instead he began with only his feelings and whatever materials were available. Sometimes he applied paints directly from the tubes to show excitement and strong feeling. He often painted in thick layers to gain a glowing effect or to cover part of an image.

Pierre-Auguste Renoir
1841–1919

Pierre-Auguste Renoir (pyâr ō gōōst´ ren wär´) was one of the most widely known and best-loved European painters. The sixth of seven children, Renoir was born into a poor family in Limoges, France. His father was a tailor, and the family had to live in a slum, with few luxuries or comforts. Renoir showed signs of talent at an early age in many artistic fields. Although he was a talented singer, he became an apprentice at a porcelain factory, where for five years he copied French masterpieces onto plates and soup tureens. During this apprenticeship Renoir developed his brushwork and his passion for the eighteenth century French master painters such as Watteau and Boucher. Renoir's work became more widely known in the 1880s, after a decade of struggle and lack of recognition.

About Art History

Renoir was one of a group of artists known as the impressionists. These artists, including Monet, Pissaro, Sisley, and Morisot, followed the advice of the poet Baudelaire to abandon historical subjects and to show the beauty of modern life instead. In attempts to record truthful and direct responses to nature they painted outside rather than inside the studio. They painted quickly in order to capture the scenes in front of their eyes before they changed. The impressionists were known for their bold, rapid technique. They covered the surfaces of their canvases with broken touches or slashes of color. The impressionists began exhibiting in 1874, and were met with extreme criticism and public hostility. Many people were unable to understand their style. Today, exhibitions of impressionist artists are greeted with much excitement.

About the Artwork

Renoir studied art for two years at the famous École des Beaux-Arts in Paris, France. He learned to draw there, but he disregarded academic guidelines that did not allow him to develop his own personal style. He discovered a new style of painting not based on the feathery brush strokes of impressionism. During this period, he also began to concentrate on using women and children as his subject matter.

About the Media
Renoir most frequently used oils or pastels.

About the Technique
Renoir painted on a white background. For the first layer of color he used paint so diluted that it ran down the canvas. Then he would cover the surface of the canvas with tiny brushstrokes of pure color.

Peter Paul Rubens
1577–1640

▲ **Peter Paul Rubens.** (Flemish). *Self-Portrait.*
c. 1638–1640.

Oil on canvas. 43 × 33½ in. (109.5 × 85 cm.).
Kunst historiches Museum, Vienna.

Peter Paul Rubens (pē´ tər pôl rōō´ bənz) grew up in Antwerp, Flanders (now Belgium). He began to study painting at a young age and practiced to be a courtier, a person of heightened social standing associated with nobility. By age 21 he was considered to be a master painter and continued creating and overseeing the production of an enormous quantity of work. Rubens was actively involved in the politics of seventeenth-century Europe, and at times helped conduct negotiations and peace treaties. His successful diplomatic efforts were recognized by Charles I of England, and the King was so impressed that he knighted the artist. Regarded as a master painter, humanist, courtier, architect, ambassador, and print designer, Rubens led a peaceful and artistically prolific life, earning the respect of dignitaries and fellow artists alike.

About Art History

In 1600, Rubens went to Venice, Italy, and was immediately inspired by the elegant coloring and forms of Titian. He also took on the styles of other Italian Renaissance painters and incorporated them into his altarpieces for the churches of Santa Croce di Gerusalemme and the Chiesa Nuova in Rome. These two pieces established a successful reputation for Rubens. He returned to Antwerp, where he set up a studio employing a team of assistants who helped him generate many religious paintings referencing the Counter-Reformation. Two of Rubens's most famous assistants were Anthony van Dyck and Frans Snyders, who were influenced by his style and later also became master painters. In his later years Rubens painted more portraits, genre scenes, and landscapes with less dogmatic fervor than his earlier work, although he continued to improve his technical skill throughout his career.

About the Artwork

Rubens's artwork combined the realistic tradition of Flemish painting with the imagination and classical themes of Italian painting. His larger works echoed his Roman Catholic faith. Although conservative, his baroque style was expressed through the use of energetic colors and light. Rubens's portrayals of Flemish peasants displayed the same sense of grace and grandeur as his 21 panels of Marie de Medici's courtly life.

About the Media

Rubens painted in oils on canvas or panel.

About the Technique

Rubens used many layers of oils and often added glazes to create luminosity.

Antonio Ruíz
1897-1964

Antonio Ruíz (an tōn´ yō roo ēs´) was born in Mexico City. He grew up in an educated family that also appreciated the arts. His grandfather was a painter, his mother a concert pianist, and his father a physician. As a child, Ruíz loved to play with construction sets. After studying art in Mexico, he moved to California, where he designed movie sets. After two years he returned to Mexico to paint and to direct children's theatre. In time, he became the director of Mexico's School of Painting and Sculpture. Ruíz also taught scenery design at the University of Mexico.

About Art History

With his wit and sophistication, Ruíz helped pull Mexican art away from ancient folklore and into the modern era. He also was influential in the area of scenery design. He designed the sets for many plays and movies.

About the Artwork

Ruíz's paintings often tell a story. For example, *The Orator* shows a small man standing on a huge chair, talking to pumpkins. In *The Shop Window*, a Mexican peasant couple gaze at blonde mannequins modeling swimsuits in a store window. The contrast between the mannequins and the peasants reflects differences between the two cultures. In his later years, Ruíz painted neat, precise pictures on small canvases, which he called *postal cards.*

About the Media

This artist painted in oils.

About the Technique

Ruíz painted slowly, completing only three or four paintings in a year. His studio was on the upper level of his house, where he would shut himself off from the world for hours. He spent so much time painting that he did not like to part with a finished piece.

John Singer Sargent
1856–1925

John Singer Sargent (jän sing´ər sär´jənt) was born to American parents, but he grew up traveling with them throughout Europe. There, he spent most of his adult life. He, along with many other Americans, earned the label *expatriate* for leading this lifestyle. Though he seldom stayed in one location for very long, he spent a long period of his career in England. Regarded as one of the most successful international society portrait artists, Sargent influenced European and American artists with his technical skills and techniques. He was such a determined artist that he painted more than 900 oils and more than 2,000 watercolors between 1877 and 1925.

About Art History

Sargent was deeply influenced by impressionist artists, the Spanish painter Velázquez, the Dutch painter Frans Hals, and his teacher Carolus-Duran. After settling for awhile in England, he became immensely famous for his portraits and his dedicated work ethic, and he was respected for his selfless efforts to help other artists. Sargent's work took on many styles and was always changing. He was regarded as an impressionist, a classical portraitist, a landscape artist, a watercolorist, a public muralist, and a sculptor.

About the Artwork

Sargent sometimes painted portraits of and for his fellow artists. This was the case with his oil painting *Daughters of Edward Darley Boit.* The painting is similar to a photograph taken with a short depth of field. Sargent painted it on a perfectly square canvas, an unusual choice that caused it to receive mixed reviews from critics.

About the Media

Among his many subjects, Sargent painted portraits of two United States presidents, as well as business tycoons, European aristocrats, and homeless children. He also painted street scenes, waterfalls, the combat lines of World War I, other artists, dancers, allegorical murals, building interiors, back alleys, and his sleeping friends. The majority of his early works were done in oils, and he shifted toward watercolors later in his career.

About the Technique

Sargent created most of his portraits from live models, often starting with a rough-painted sketch that he finalized later. For landscapes, he traveled throughout the country looking for the perfect scene. On one sketching tour, he hiked throughout the Rocky Mountains in the pouring rain to paint landscapes with waterfalls.

Miriam Schapiro
b. 1923

Miriam Schapiro (mir´ ē əm shə pir´ ō) is an American artist who was born in Toronto, Canada. She grew up in the Flatbush section of Brooklyn, New York. Her parents encouraged her pursuit of a career in art and sent her to art classes at the Museum of Modern Art. She met her husband, artist Paul Brach, while attending college. They married in 1946 and have a son who is a writer. Schapiro organizes her home life so that art is woven into it. She can move from baking in the kitchen to painting in her studio and back to the kitchen without feeling interrupted. Her husband says that she has learned to live a "seamless life."

About Art History

In the beginning of Schapiro's career, her work was abstract expressionistic. Later she became an important leader in the feminist art movement of the early 1970s. She wanted art to speak as a woman speaks. In art history, women's art has been hidden. Even the materials that women have used—lace, fabric, tea towels, ribbon, sequins, buttons, rickrack, yarn, silk, cotton, and so on—have been left out of art history.

About the Artwork

In time, Schapiro's work became more geometric and structured. In the 1950s, she expressed her identity by including feminist themes in her art. In 1972, Schapiro and other female artists changed an old Hollywood mansion into a totally female environment and called it "womanhouse." Schapiro and Sherry Brody made *The Dollhouse*— a construction of bits of fabric and tiny household objects meant to reflect female life and fantasy. Schapiro also made "femmages." She and a few other artists invented this word to describe art made with techniques that women traditionally use, such as sewing, embroidery, piecework, and appliqué. *Femmages* are collages that reflect female emotions and creativity.

About the Media

Schapiro uses fabric scraps, sequins, buttons, threads, rickrack, spangles, yarn, silk, taffeta, cotton, burlap, wool, and other materials a person might use in daily life.

About the Technique

Schapiro uses collage, assemblage, and decoupage to join materials.

▲ **John Scholl.** (American). *Sunburst.* 1907–1916.

Painted on wood with wire on metal. 71 × 38 × 24$\frac{1}{2}$ inches (180.3 × 96.5 × 62.2 cm.). American Folk Art Museum, New York, New York.

John Scholl
1827–1916

John Scholl (jän shōl) was born in Würtemburg, Germany, and immigrated to the United States in 1853. He settled in the forested region of Germania, Pennsylvania, and worked as a builder. Some of his constructions included his own house and additional houses, the village church, the local brewery, and the general store. Scholl received no artistic training, but when he retired at the age of eighty, he began to create hand-carved, decorative wooden objects that now sell for thousands of dollars at folk art auctions. He did not carve for commercial reasons, and he never sold any of his work. Until 1967, his entire collection remained together and in the possession of his children and grandchildren.

About Art History

Scholl's art is characterized as both folk and naive art, and it is often difficult to tell the difference between the two styles. Naive artists are generally self-taught and make works that can be identified by altered perspective or a fresh, new use of color. Although they usually lack artistic training, naive artists are not necessarily uneducated people. Where *folk art* is typically based on specific tradition, *naive art* tends to be more eccentric and uses innovative themes. Scholl's work can be seen as folk art for its adherence to German folk design, but it can also be viewed as naive art for its colorful originality.

About the Artwork

Scholl's subjects originated from traditional Pennsylvania German motifs, including the dove, bird-of-paradise, tulip, anchor, peacock, star-crossed circle, and swan. He typically embellished his works with his own unique Victorian *fretwork,* a style of decoration characteristic of gingerbread motifs. Tulip imagery holds an interesting place in German and Dutch history, as well as in Pennsylvania Dutch and German folk art. Introduced to Germany in 1559, the tulip became instantly popular in trading, farming, literature, and art. It was originally the symbol of love in Persia, where it was honored in tulip festivals. When it arrived with German and Dutch settlers in the United States in the nineteenth century, the tulip became a traditional decoration on the front of houses, in art, on furniture, and in household wares.

About the Media

Whimsical wooden carvings make up the 50 known pieces of Scholl's art. For example, *Sunburst* is made from painted wood, wire, and metal.

About the Technique

Scholl carved each of his works by hand using only a jackknife. He painted some of them in bright colors and designs, often accentuating the carved patterns with patterns of color.

Leo Sewell
b. 1945

Leo Sewell (lē´ ō soo´ əl) grew up in Annapolis, Maryland, near a dump. His parents always challenged him to be creative, so he began making art with a few simple tools and the things he collected from the junkyard. His early, simple pieces eventually progressed into elaborate, decorative sculptures that have been exhibited throughout the world. His artwork can be found in children's museums and large corporations, and he also creates commissioned work. Sewell's studio is in Philadelphia, Pennsylvania.

About Art History

In 1968, Sewell decided to make junk sculpture, but supplemented his income with other jobs until 1985, when he became a full-time sculptor. He refers to his artistic aesthetic as *horror vacui,* which is Latin for "fear of nothing." This historical art term explains that the human eye is afraid of seeing plainness, so Sewell fills his art with as many layers of objects as possible, often relating his found elements specifically to the sculpted subject. Artists working in movements such as Dadaism and futurism also used found objects.

About the Artwork

Dogs, penguins, people, and dinosaurs are sculptures Sewell has made using his junkyard assemblage technique. He chooses objects and materials based on their color, shape, texture, and durability, and he has created sculptures ranging in size from a life-sized cat to a 24-foot *Stegosaurus.* One of the challenges he encounters when constructing these found-object creations is making sure that the materials he uses will not deteriorate over time or fall apart with age. He is constantly visiting junkyards to add to his collection of found materials and to generate inspiration for further work.

About the Media

The media in Sewell's collection include wood, metal, plastic, steel, aluminum, brass, and stainless steel. Recently he has incorporated soldered sterling silver into his sculptures.

About the Technique

Once he has an idea, Sewell joins his discarded materials with nails, bolts, and screws. He welds metal objects together for outdoor sculptures.

Sandy Skoglund
b. 1946

Sandy Skoglund (san´ dē skōg lund´) spent the first part of her childhood near Boston and then moved around the United States with her family. She had polio when she was young, and the time she spent indoors cultivated her passion for drawing. Her drawings often depicted fantasy lands and environments. These early imaginations have filtered into her work today with installations that create entirely new environments with fantastic elements, such as walls of jam and floors of eggshells. Skoglund has been an undergraduate professor at Rutgers University and credits her students with keeping her in touch with the world outside the New York art scene.

About Art History

In college Skoglund developed a fascination for art history and the academic pursuit of art's meaning. This education encouraged her to think about herself as an artist and the relationship between American culture and European culture as expressed in art. In the 1970s she began evaluating this cultural difference in her installations, and she continues to use elaborate masses of material to depict excessive American behavior. Many artists have inspired Skoglund, including Claes Oldenburg, George Segal, Edward and Nancy Kienholz, Paul Thek, and installation artist Ann Hamilton.

About the Artwork

In her earlier work Skoglund used bright colors. She believes an artist should make use of a wide range of materials that explore color and texture. Her work involves the viewer's sense of smell, taste, and familiarity with fabric textures. Each of these senses was engaged in her installation *The Cocktail Party*, in which an entire room—its contents, and its inhabitants—were covered in neon orange cheese puffs. Skoglund creates installations that she then

photographs, and her photograph of *The Cocktail Party* shows both mannequins and live people draped in the repetitive crescent-shaped texture of the crunchy snack food.

About the Media

Skoglund's installations tend to use perishable materials such as raw hamburger, strawberry jam, honey, raw bacon, eggshells, and cheese puffs, so she uses photography to document her work.

About the Technique

Skoglund begins an installation by gathering materials and experimenting with their sculptural aspects, and then she writes ideas in a notebook based on the inspiration she finds in her materials. Skoglund works with assistants to produce her pieces, although some of the installations are portable, allowing the artist to take photos of her constructed space and then reassemble its panels in a new location. For *The Cocktail Party* she used a hot glue gun to attach each cheese puff to the walls, floor, mannequins, and clothing.

Jaune Quick-to-See Smith

b. 1941

Jaune Quick-to-See Smith (zhōn kwik tōo sē smith) was born into a large family on a Montana reservation. She often went hungry as a child. Her Shoshone grandmother gave her the name "Quick-to-See" because Smith was quick to understand things. When Smith was in first grade, she already knew she wanted to be an artist. Later she was told that she was not college material and that a woman could not have a career in art. Smith spent 22 years supporting herself, raising three children, finishing college, and completing a master's degree in painting. She now paints as frequently as possible in a remodeled stable behind her home in New Mexico. When she is not painting, she lectures, teaches, and serves as a guest artist at colleges across the nation. Smith has been featured in magazines and several documentaries.

About Art History

Smith combines techniques used by abstract expressionist painters with images from her Native American background. Some galleries rejected Smith's modern paintings because they were not "Indian enough." For this reason, Smith arranges regular exhibits for young Native American artists. She wants these artists to be able to exhibit their work no matter what their subjects include.

About the Artwork

Smith's work expresses her concern about the destruction of the environment and of Native American cultures. In *Forest*, for example, a real handsaw in the painting suggests the future destruction of trees. In *Trade Gifts for Trading Land with White People*, she combined real souvenirs from sports teams that were named using Native American terms such as *Braves* and *Indians*. To Smith, the souvenirs and team names show a lack of respect for Native American cultures.

About the Media

Smith most frequently integrates real objects, such as ropes, nails, and spoons, and oil paints.

About the Technique

Smith adds texture to her paintings by pasting pieces of fabric and paper onto the canvas and painting over them. She blends colors with her hand.

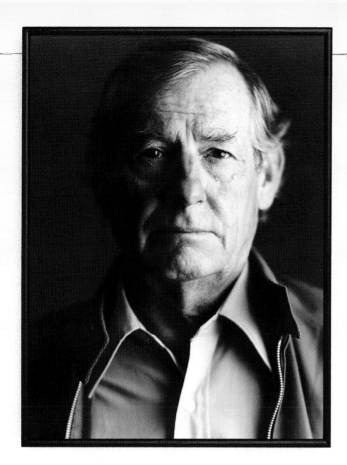

Wayne Thiebaud

b. 1920

Wayne Thiebaud (wān tē´ bō), one of California's most famous contemporary painters, has earned as many awards for excellence in teaching as he has for his painting and printmaking. He became interested in drawing in high school and later worked as a freelance cartoonist and illustrator. He continued his artwork during his military service in the U.S. Air Force during World War II. He drew cartoons for the military base newspaper. In 1949 Thiebaud decided to become a painter. His first one-person show in New York City was praised by the critics. At that time his subjects were mass-produced consumer goods, particularly junk food, and he was mistakenly classified with the pop artists. Later, he was classified as an American realist. His primary interest is organizing realistic subject matter into abstract compositions.

About Art History

Thiebaud arrived on the New York art scene in the 1960s when pop art was developing. He is sometimes identified as a pop artist because of the subject matter in much of his work. For example, many of his works show such objects as pinball machines, lipstick, and food. Thiebaud started as a realistic painter but later simplified his work, making it more abstract.

About the Artwork

Thiebaud reduces shapes to simple forms in his city landscapes. The viewer can easily identify circles, squares, triangles, rectangles, and arcs.

About the Media

Thiebaud paints with oils and acrylics, and creates a variety of prints.

About the Technique

Thiebaud tested mixing acrylic paint with oil paint, but he found that the mixture dissolved. He then tried painting oils over acrylics and discovered that he could achieve the effects he wanted. Before beginning to paint, Thiebaud stares at an object for a long time. Then he changes and adapts the object until it is the way he wants it in his painting.

Joaquin Torres-Garcia
1874–1949

Joaquin Torres-Garcia (wäh kēn´ tor´ res gär sē´ ä) was born in Uruguay. His family moved to Spain when he was 17 years old. An eager student and deep thinker, he studied many subjects, including art. As a young man, Torres-Garcia illustrated magazines, created murals, and taught art classes to support himself. In 1915 Torres-Garcia designed wooden toys with interchangeable parts to amuse his three children. He moved to New York City, where he hoped to sell the toys. However, they were difficult to manufacture. After trying to sell his toys in Italy, Torres-Garcia and his family settled in Paris. He began to use abstract primitive figures in his paintings and sold many of them. He then moved back to Uruguay and opened a successful art school. He also wrote and published articles and books, including an autobiography.

About Art History

Torres-Garcia helped found Cercle et Carre (Circle and Square), a group of artists in Paris. The group held exhibitions and published reviews of abstract art. In his own work, Torres-Garcia combined elements of the ancient pre-Columbian art of South America with elements of modern European art.

About the Artwork

Early in his career, Torres-Garcia painted realistic landscapes and murals. In time his work became more abstract and was organized by vertical and horizontal lines. Torres-Garcia filled his paintings with signs and symbols representing people, places, and ideas. He even invented his own alphabet and used it in some of his work.

About the Media

Torres-Garcia worked in oils, watercolors, and ink. He also created murals, wooden sculptural pieces, and toys.

About the Technique

Torres-Garcia was fascinated with structure. He used lines and color to organize his paintings. Sometimes he drew grids over his paintings to divide them into sections.

Patssi Valdez

b. 1951

Patssi Valdez was born in California and grew up in Los Angeles, where she became involved in politically active performance art. Her present work includes large, brightly colored paintings that address themes of self-realization and the borderline between an inner personal world and a vibrant public world. She often paints rooms with expressive patterns and movement, drawing attention to windows or doors that look out on a richly colored landscape.

About Art History

Valdez's artistic career began with her involvement in the Chicano and Chicana art movements of the 1970s and 1980s. She became a founding member of the conceptual performance group *ASCO,* which is also the Spanish word for "nausea." ASCO challenged stereotypical images of culture and promoted political activism as a means for social empowerment. After attending the Otis Parsons School of Design, Valdez began using her work to explore the concepts of self-renewal and self-examination, and to examine references to dream, memory, and experience.

About the Artwork

Much of Valdez's art deals with themes of change and personal development, as well as traditional themes of altars, virgins, queens, and goddesses. Images of domestic space also occur in her work, including living rooms, dining rooms, kitchens, and bedrooms with dreamlike perspectives and angles. She uses the recurring imagery of drapery and theatre curtains to frame many of her compositions,

giving her everyday environments an added sense of dramatic vision. In *The Magic Room* Valdez used bold colors to depict swirling floors and flying chairs amid a room of tilting walls with dizzying patterns. The contrast of a personal domestic interior that has been transformed into a public stage echoes the way many Hispanic artists feel both a collective identity and a separation of self in the contemporary art world.

About the Media

At the beginning of her career, Valdez created performance art, installations, photographs, graphic arts, and costume and stage design. She now focuses on expressing her voice through acrylic paintings that incorporate a gentler, more subdued palette.

▲ **Rembrandt van Rijn.** (Dutch). *Self-Portrait.* 1629.
Oil on panel. $35\frac{1}{3} \times 25$ inches (89.7 × 73.5 cm.).
Isabella Stewart Gardner Museum, Boston, Massachusetts.

Rembrandt van Rijn
1606–1669

Rembrandt van Rijn (rem´ brandt vän rīn´) was the most influential Dutch artist of the seventeenth century. The seventh of nine children born to a miller and his wife, Rembrandt showed talent early in life. His parents took great interest in providing him with an education despite their modest income. Rembrandt studied a short time at the Leiden Latin School in the Netherlands to prepare for a profession as a city administrator. His parents eventually removed him from school and placed him in apprenticeships with painters. After moving to Amsterdam in 1631, he gained the commissions of several wealthy patrons and achieved great success. Rembrandt spent a large portion of the money he earned at auctions and his personal art collection. He encountered turbulent times both personally and financially, but he continued to produce works of art until his death in 1669.

About Art History

Most painters during the 1600s traveled to Italy to study art. Italian art and artists such as Michelangelo and Raphael were highly esteemed at this time. Rembrandt chose to remain in the Netherlands to learn about art. His remarkable ability to show feeling and emotion through dramatic lighting has made his work universally understandable and appreciated. Rembrandt is considered one of the greatest Western artists from all periods and countries.

About the Artwork

Under the painter Pieter Lastman, Rembrandt learned how to create dramatic accents using light and shadow, gesture, expression, and composition. In all, Rembrandt created more than 600 paintings as well as a large number of drawings, etchings, and more than 60 self-portraits. He most frequently created portraits, but he also completed paintings with historical, biblical, and mythological themes.

About the Media

Rembrandt worked mainly in oils on wood and canvas. He completed drawings on paper with pen and ink and also created etchings.

About the Technique

Rembrandt used a technique called *chiaroscuro,* an Italian word meaning "light and dark." He used light to focus attention on certain areas that contained details and left other parts in shadows using dark colors.

Paolo Veronese

1528–1588

Born Paolo Caliari in Verona, Italy, the name *Paolo Veronese* (pä´ ō lō   ver ə nā´ sē) was created from the city of his birth. When he was 14, Veronese was apprenticed to a Venetian painter, and by the time he was in his early twenties, he was painting at the Palazzo Ducale. Veronese worked in Venice and other nearby towns for the rest of life. He operated a workshop in Venice, and hired his brothers and sons. After his death Veronese's family continued to make works under the label *Haeredes Pauli,* making it difficult for historians to discern whether Veronese was the true artist behind some works.

▲ **Artist unknown.** (Italian).
Paolo Veronese. c 1560.

About Art History

Veronese painted in the mannerist style. Mannerism rejected calm balance in favor of emotion and distortion, and it idealized the works of Michelangelo and Raphael. Unlike these artists, however, painters in Venice were known for their use of color and for preferring shapes and patterns to line. Mannerists tended to paint muscular figures in complicated poses. Influential mannerists included Rosso Fiorentino, Pontormo, and Parmigianino.

About the Artwork

Veronese is famous for his enormous scenes showing religious, mythological, and allegorical subject matter. He also created portraits and decorations for the homes of the wealthy.

About the Media

Veronese worked primarily with oil paints on canvas.

About the Technique

Veronese used drawings and oil sketches to prepare for his paintings. When creating oil paintings, he would first lay out the composition, apply middle tones, and finally add the highlights and shadows.

Andrea del Verrocchio

1435–1488

Andrea del Verrocchio (än drā´ ə del və rô´ kē ō) was a Florentine sculptor during the early Italian Renaissance. He was born Andrea di Cione, and he took the name Verrocchio from the master in his first apprenticeship, Giuliano Verrocchi. Originally a goldsmith, the artist eventually became a sculptor, and also did some painting. His family was rarely financially secure, so he supported several of his brothers and sisters through the sale of his artwork. Later he provided the funds for the education of his younger brother's children. Verrocchio never married. Instead he immersed himself in the creation of his studio and workshop and stayed in Florence almost all his life.

About Art History

A student of the early Renaissance master Filippo Lippi, Verrocchio was considered to be the leading sculptor of his time; many important artists of the late fifteenth century studied with him. His impressive list of students includes Leonardo da Vinci, Perugino, Domenico Ghirlandaio, and Lorenzo di Credi. Verrocchio's most famous works were created during the last 20 years of his life, and the influential political leaders Lorenzo and Pierro de Medici were his prominent patrons during this time. They commissioned paintings and sculptures from him, as well as costumes and decorative armor for their festivals, tournaments, and receptions. Verrocchio became the curator for the Medici collection of antiquities, and he restored many pieces of ancient Roman sculpture.

About the Artwork

Although he painted, Verrocchio's true mastery lay in his three-dimensional creations. Verrocchio's *David* is one of his earliest and most graceful bronze sculptures. It depicts a youthful David with his shoulders back and a confident grin, standing victorious over the slain head of Goliath. The boy's lithe body and elegant limbs are characteristic of the elongated figures created by Verrocchio.

About the Media

Verrocchio created his sculptures from both marble and cast bronze.

About the Technique

Verrocchio planned a process of subtraction. He began with large blocks of solid marble, which he would carve and whittle away into the smooth forms of his figures.

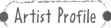

James McNeill Whistler

1834–1903

Although James McNeill Whistler (jāmz mǝk nēl´ hwis´ lǝr) was born in Lowell, Massachusetts, he often claimed that he was born somewhere in Europe. Whistler did spend part of his childhood in Russia—his father, an engineer, helped construct the St. Petersburg-Moscow railroad—and he studied at the Imperial Academy of Fine Arts for one year. After returning to America, Whistler attended West Point Military Academy, and then he traveled to Paris to study art. Throughout his career Whistler worked experimentally and refused to be associated with any one style of painting.

▲ **James McNeill Whistler.** (American).
Arrangement in Gray: Portrait of the Painter. c. 1872.

Oil on canvas. 29 × 21 inches (74.9 × 53.3 cm.).
The Detroit Institute of Arts, Detroit, Michigan.

About Art History

When Whistler first went to Paris, the city's artists were divided between traditional styles and the radical ideas of artists, such as Courbet, who said artists should paint what seems relevant. Whistler painted at the studio of Charles Gleyre, where he was encouraged to experiment. In 1859, Whistler moved to London where he was influenced by the *pre-Raphaelites,* a group of English artists who wished to recapture the beauty of the medieval world, and the *impressionists,* who felt that artists should paint directly from nature. He strongly believed in the aesthetic principle of creating art for its own sake.

About the Artwork

Whistler painted many outdoor scenes and portraits, but for much of his life he insisted that an artwork's subject did not matter. He believed his art should be aesthetically pleasing and not emotionally charged. Whistler is best known for his paintings and drawings, but he also designed color schemes for rooms and decorated furniture and houses.

About the Media

Whistler used oil paints, watercolors, pen and ink, and pastels.

About the Technique

As Whistler moved away from realism toward a more aesthetic style, he began to use thinner layers of paint and fewer colors in his paintings. Whistler sometimes used a Parisian "memory method," by which he would study a scene and draw it from memory. Later he chose to paint directly from nature.

Grant Wood

1892–1942

Grant Wood (grant wŏŏd) was born in Iowa and lived there most of his life. His father died when Wood was ten years old. When he was 14 he won third prize in a national Crayola contest by coloring a leaf. He studied drawing and design after high school. As a soldier in World War I, he designed artillery camouflage. After the war, Wood taught art in several high schools and studied art during multiple trips to Europe. In 1927, he retired from teaching high school to paint full-time. Later he served as the Iowa director of the Public Works Art Project. He taught at the University of Iowa and lectured across the nation.

About Art History

During his trips to Europe, Wood tried different painting styles, such as impressionism and primitive painting. His own realistic style emerged in *American Gothic,* the painting that made Wood famous. He became one of the leaders of the regionalism movement of the 1930s.

About the Artwork

Wood believed that artists should paint from their own experiences in their home communities. For this reason, Wood painted mainly landscapes of Iowa and farm scenes. In *Dinner for Threshers,* for example, he showed farm workers in overalls gathered around a dining table. Wood also painted murals, illustrated Sinclair Lewis's novel *Main Street,* and completed a cover for *Time* magazine.

About the Media

Wood worked in oils, pencil, charcoal, watercolors, and chalk. He also created lithographs.

About the Technique

Wood's painting technique changed over the years. He began work on his best-known paintings by carefully creating sketches and oil studies. When he was ready to begin painting, he covered the canvas with one layer of paint. He then transferred his detailed drawing to the canvas with small brushstrokes. He finished his work with glazes, which are translucent layers of color.

Malcah Zeldis
b. 1931

Folk painter Malcah Zeldis (mal´ kə zel´ dəs) was born in New York and grew up in Detroit. Her family was originally from Russia, and at the age of 17 she went to live in Israel for ten years, where she taught herself to paint. She uses her artwork to express admiration for her Jewish heritage and people of all faiths and ethnicities. Zeldis has illustrated a number of children's books and fills her paintings with an optimistic view of life that celebrates the diversity of America.

About Art History

While living in Israel, Zeldis worked on a Kibbutz, which is an Israeli collective settlement that holds all property and wealth in common. In addition to learning how to paint, she was married in Israel and returned to New York in 1958. Her husband discouraged her painting, and in 1974, they divorced. Once independent Zeldis was able to devote herself to her art, and she was quickly recognized by establishments such as the Museum of American Folk Art, the National Museum of American Art, and the Jewish Museum. She was the first living artist to have a retrospective exhibition at the Museum of American Folk Art in New York, and she continues to paint in New York today.

About the Artwork

Zeldis's paintings are packed with brightly colored people compressed into a shallow picture plane. She often includes images of her favorite historic figures, such as Abraham Lincoln, Martin Luther King Jr., Elvis Presley, Moses, and Marilyn Monroe, and she sometimes includes herself in her crowded scenes. In *Miss Liberty Celebration*, Zeldis fills her composition with swarms of diverse people, and she painted the symbol of freedom as a reference to her liberation from cancer. Her creations act as visual narratives, exploding with color and energy, and she applies great detail to her abstract forms.

About the Media

When Zeldis had cancer she was too weak to lift heavy masonite for her paintings, so she began to paint in oils on lightweight corrugated cardboard she found on her street.

About the Technique

Zeldis does not use academic rules or formats in her painting. Instead she designs her forms using her own imagination and self-taught skill.

Basket

This basket was made by an unidentified western Apache artist at the beginning of the twentieth century. Many Apache artisans of this time made baskets specifically to sell to tourists. They did not sign their work or indicate their identity on these baskets, so it is impossible to know exactly who made any particular piece. It is believed that this basket was made by a member of the Western Apache Tonto group of the southwestern United States.

◀ **Artist unknown.** (Western Apache/North America). *Basket.* c. 1900.

Willow, devil's claw, wood. 28 inches (71.1 cm.). Detroit Art Institute, Detroit, Michigan.

About Art History

Tonto Apache and other Native American tribal groups have made baskets for practical and ceremonial purposes for thousands of years. Toward the end of the nineteenth century, tourists, collectors, and retail shops began to take an interest in buying handmade baskets from Native American peoples. Apache artists developed new styles of baskets made specifically for sale to tourists and retail shops. This basket is an example of a type of jar-shaped basket called an *olla* that was made for sale to a collector.

About the Artwork

This basket is quite large; its height is approximately 28 inches. A beautiful pattern is woven in the contrasting colors of the willow shoots and the devil's claw roots. The surface is smooth and beautifully crafted. This basket has some characteristics of the older style Apache baskets of the pre-Depression era, when many traditional art forms and techniques were abandoned due to harsh economic conditions that forced many Native American artisans into factory work and other kinds of wage labor.

About the Media

This basket was made from willow twigs, slender roots from the devil's claw plant, and wooden sticks.

About the Technique

Apache artists made this type of jar-shaped basket by weaving flexible young willow shoots around a basic three-rod frame made from pieces of wood. The willow shoots are stripped of their bark, revealing the pale young wood beneath. This basket also includes the thin roots of the devil's claw plant, which provides the dark color in the pattern. The smooth, compact, uniform layers of the basket's coils indicate high-quality weaving.

Canister

This canister was made by a Pennsylvania Dutch artisan. In 1683 the first German-speaking colonists arrived in the New World to settle William Penn's colony of Pennsylvania. Many of them, such as the Quakers, the Mennonites, the Amish, and the Moravians, were escaping religious persecution. Pennsylvania offered religious freedom for settlers from various levels of society. They included university graduates, highly skilled craftspeople, and farmers.

◀ **Artist unknown.** (United States). *Canister.* 1825.
....
Tin. American Folk Art Museum, New York, New York.

About Art History

The Pennsylvania Dutch often decorated objects with great care and skill. Their works took many forms, including tinware, pottery, Steigel glass, tombstones, clocks, and carved and painted woodenware.

About the Artwork

The Pennsylvania Dutch used tin to make a great variety of household objects, including trays, boxes, watering cans, flowerpots, canisters, and candleholders. Decorations were painted in rich reds, rust tones, yellow ocher, tan, and green. Birds, hearts, tulips, people, and patriotic motifs such as the American flag and eagle were common decorative themes.

About the Media

Mallets, shears, and molds were used to create tinware forms. Dyes extracted from roots, berries, tree barks, nutshells, and other plant parts were used to make colored pigments. Brushes, cardboard, varnish, and natural paints were used to design the objects.

About the Technique

Pennsylvania Dutch tinware was made of thin sheets of iron dipped into molten tin. In the early years, most tinware was painted freehand with bold C-strokes, S-strokes, curlicues, wavy strokes, and spiraling tendril lines. A stenciling technique was later developed to create these designs.

Ceremonial Shield

The Solomon Islands are a group of volcanic islands in the South Pacific located 1,500 miles north of Sydney, Australia. The inhabitants are Melanesian and Polynesian, and they speak a Malayo-Polynesian language. Polynesian society is based on a political organization headed by chiefs. The art usually serves to uphold spiritual power, or *mana*.

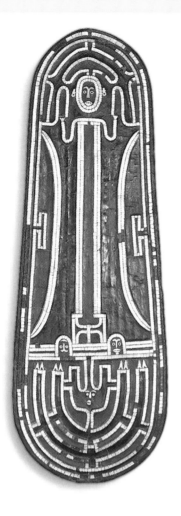

◀ **Artist unknown.** (Melanesia).
Ceremonial Shield. c. 1852.

Basketry, nautilus shell inlay on resin base. $32\frac{5}{8} \times 9\frac{1}{4}$ inches (82.86 × 23.5 cm.). The Brooklyn Museum, Brooklyn, New York.

About Art History

The Solomon Islands were discovered in 1567 by Spanish explorer Alvaro de Mendana de Neira. In 1893, the South Solomon islands were placed under English protection. Germany gave the North Solomons to England in 1900. The capital of the island group called *Honiara* is on Guadalcanal.

About the Artwork

This piece of rare and intricately designed artwork was collected by Captain James Booth of the British Navy. It was probably made around 1852. It is a piece typifying the artwork created in the Solomon Islands and New Guinea. The long human figure takes up most of the space on the shield. The features are stylized; they are composed of lines and shapes that imitate a realistic appearance. Standard war shields from the Solomon Islands were plain and oval shaped. These shields were not used in battle. They were probably a status symbol for men of high rank.

About the Media

This ceremonial shield is made from basketry with a nautilus shell inlay on a resin base.

About the Technique

The artist painted the basketry work black and red and made the design with pieces of shell inlay. The black paint helps the red areas stand out. The artist cut shallow holes into the wood and inserted the stones and nautilus shells into these holes.

Egyptian Cat

Ancient Egypt was ruled by pharaohs, and every pharaoh had hundreds of servants. Many artists in Egypt were servants of the pharaohs. This cat sculpture probably was made by one of these royal artisans.

◀ **Artist unknown.** (Egypt). *Egyptian Cat.* Late Dynasty.

Bronze. $4\frac{3}{4} \times 3$ inches (12 × 7.6 cm.). The Metropolitan Museum of Art, New York, New York.

About Art History

The ancient Egyptians started keeping cats as pets around 3500 B.C., the first people to do this. They liked cats because cats were good rodent hunters. The Egyptians believed that cats were sacred, so no one was allowed to kill a cat. When some cats died, they were made into mummies and buried in special tombs.

About the Artwork

Animals were popular subjects in Egyptian art. The Egyptians believed that many animals had supernatural powers. They believed that cats were especially powerful. Small statues, like this cat, were often put into tombs and graves to protect the dead and to hunt mice. This cat sculpture was created sometime between 950 B.C. and 300 B.C.

About the Media

This sculpture is made of bronze. Bronze is a metal made from a mixture of copper and tin.

About the Technique

Bronze sculptures are made through a process called *casting*. The artist first creates a mold, then pours melted bronze into it. When the bronze cools and is hardened, the mold is removed. The sculpture is then polished.

Figure from House Post

The Maori people settled in New Zealand during the neolithic stone age. The importance of individuals in Maori society was determined by birth order and gender. Firstborn sons inherited leadership roles. Land, canoes, and houses were communal property. Personal possessions were limited to clothes, weapons, and a few other items.

◀ **Artist Unknown.** (Maori, New Zealand). *Figure from House Post.* Nineteenth century.
....
Wood. 43 inches (109.2 cm. tall).
The Metropolitan Museum of Art, New York, New York.

About Art History

The Maori used bone, ivory, stone, and wood for carvings and sculptures. The carvings and sculptures were freestanding *tiki* (ancestral spirit figures), house panels, and canoes. Artists added surface patterns by cutting grooves, notches, and lines, and by painting. The Maori were also weavers who used different types of soft fabrics to create patterns featuring images from the natural world, such as coconut palms and feathers.

About the Artwork

Most Maori carvings are impersonal and stylized. Some, like the one shown here, have realistic heads and abstract bodies. In Maori cultures, tattoo patterns identified a man more than the features of his face. These tattoo patterns represented particular ancestors and great people in tribal history. The individual ancestral figure carvings appeared in rows, forming the panels of meeting houses, which were regarded as places where spirits could dwell and protect the living.

About the Media

In Maori tradition, trees provided a home for the offspring of the gods—birds, people, and all other creatures. Woodcarvers often used the coniferous totara tree, which was easy to find and split into log slabs. It was soft enough to cut and chisel. The totara was durable, but developed surface cracks when exposed to sun and rain. The great Kauri pine provided finer wood for carving, but was much more difficult to find.

About the Technique

Surface patterns were added to the sculpted form. Surface decorations varied, but the range of cuts that could be made with stone-age tools was limited. This technical limitation determined the range of spirals, notches, zigzag lines, crescents, and ridges that could be formed.

Jaguar

The Aztecs believed in supernatural forces. Their artists were in charge of creating the mythical and religious images used in rituals and daily life. The artists held some power because it was believed that they could materialize gods and spirits in stone. Judging from the style of this jaguar, it was likely carved in a major city by an Aztec carver who worked in a workshop of carvers.

▲ **Artist unknown.** (Aztec/Mexico). *Jaguar.*
1440–1852.

Stone. $4\frac{15}{16} \times 11\frac{1}{16}$ inches (12.5 × 14.5 × 28 cm.).
The Brooklyn Museum, Brooklyn, New York.

About Art History

The life span of the Aztec civilization was short. For most of their history, they wandered throughout southern Mexico as nomads. In the 1400s they built their first cities. The most famous was Tenochtitlán. Within 100 years, the Aztecs were invaded by a Spanish expedition led by Cortez. Although the Spanish tore down Aztec temples, enough Aztec architecture and sculpture survives to give historians an idea of how their society functioned.

About the Artwork

The jaguar here symbolizes the Aztec god Tezcatlipoca. He was often represented as a jaguar, although he could take on many forms. Tezcatlipoca was the god of night, of the moon, and of destruction. The jaguar was the most feared animal in the Mexican jungle. The jaguar also represented the Aztec king. This stone jaguar was either used in ceremonies involving a ritual feast, or it rested in the king's court.

About the Media

The Aztecs carved much of their statuary from volcanic rock, which is soft and easy to shape. Like this jaguar, some of the small pieces were cut from dense stone common to the jungle hills of Mexico. The knives they used were made from volcanic glass. To polish the stone, the Aztecs used coarse stone and fine sand.

About the Technique

Before the Aztecs began carving a stone, they smashed it down to the desired size. Next they slowly carved away the stone grain with sharp, volcanic glass knives. To give the jaguar its polished look, the carvers rubbed sand and abrasive stones along its surface.

Standing Ruler

The kingdom of the Mayan people covered a large geographic area of what today is called Central America and southern Mexico. Historians can date evidence of the Mayan culture back to 700 B.C. The ancient Maya had a complex written language, many unique forms of art and architecture, sophisticated methods of producing crops, accurate calendars and other methods of keeping time, and an impressive knowledge of astronomy and other sciences. The Maya were spiritual people who believed in a supernatural world and worshipped gods that appeared to be part human and part animal.

◀ **Artist unknown.** (Mayan). *Standing Ruler.* c. 600-800 A.D.

Ceramic with traces of paint. $9\frac{1}{2}$ inches (24.13 cm.) high. Kimbell Art Museum, Fort Worth Texas.

About Art History

Portraits of important rulers were one of the main art forms in ancient Mayan culture. Rulers were depicted standing or sitting in regal poses, wearing the clothing and symbolic ornamentation that distinguished them from other nobles of the period. Patterns and symbols woven into a ruler's clothing gave information about his accomplishments, his family associations, and his position within the society. Elaborate headdresses bore spiritual symbols pertaining to Mayan beliefs about connections between the physical world and a supernatural world of gods and animal spirits.

About the Artwork

The statue *Standing Ruler* was created by a Mayan sculptor sometime between 600 A.D. and 800 A.D., during what is known as the classic period. The name of the ruler is not known, but his position as royalty is made clear by his headdress and other effects. The statue probably was meant to be an official portrait of this ruler, honoring him with its depiction of the figure in the full regalia of war and ritual ceremonies.

About the Media

Portrait statues were often made of clay, which is easy to harvest from the dense clay soils of Central American regions. Traces of paint evident on the statue were also made from minerals and plants found in the area.

About the Technique

After the clay sculpture was formed by hand, it was fired in a kiln. After it was cooled, the figure was painted with colorful pigments that have maintained their rich hues for centuries.

Yeihl Nax'in Raven Screen

The Tlingit live in the heavily forested and damp coastal islands of southeastern Alaska. They live in large, cedar-planked communal houses filled with carvings and paintings that express the power and prestige of the inhabitants. These symbols are displayed at great feasts called *potlatches*. In Tlingit society, shamans used carvings and paintings as part of their rituals. Shamans were buried with such ritual objects.

▲ **Artist unknown (Tlingit).** (United States). *Yeihl Nax'in Raven Screen.* c. 1830.

Spruce and paint. $8\frac{13}{16} \times 10\frac{3}{4}$ feet. (2.69 × 3.8 meters). The Seattle Art Museum, Seattle, Washington.

About Art History

The Tlingit created crests for their houses. Crests tell about a clan's history, status, and destiny. Crest animals include wolves, eagles, bears, and killer whales. They were visual symbols of the social order. *Yek* were supernatural animals and were thought to be controlled by shamans. These animals include salmon, frogs, and halibut.

About the Artwork

House partitions, or screens, were located in the backs of communal houses and provided privacy to the house leader, *Hit'saati*, and his family. This screen design shows a black raven in an upright position. The raven's legs and other design areas are red. The Hit'saati is the human counterpart of the raven. In Tlingit tradition, ravens and humans share many characteristics. Ravens represent intelligence, playfulness, and protection of territory.

About the Media

The Tlingit used wood to make many things, including hair combs, shaman carvings, and sculptures. Sometimes *yek* were carved at the bottoms of the ornamental pieces. The original paints of this house partition were covered when it was repainted in 1898.

About the Technique

The Tlingit used spruce and paint to create this screen. They created paint from many different sources. Black paint was created from graphite or charcoal mixed with dried salmon eggs. Red paint was made using Chinese vermillion the Tlingit obtained through trading. Blue was made from copper minerals. Paint was applied with bear fur or porcupine-quill brushes.